D0007516

# MARIGOLD MORNINGS

*a family love story*

# DOROTHY EVSLIN

Christian Herald House
40 Overlook Drive, Chappaqua, New York

To my cast as they appeared: Bud, Tom, Bill, Pamela, Janet, Micki, TomBurbank, Darlene, Tanya, Meir, Galeal, Jarah, and the little one who is expected in January.

God setteth the solitary in families . . .

—Psalm 68:6 KJV

The year's at the spring
And day's at the morn;
Morning's at seven;
The hillside's dew-pearled;
The lark's on the wing;
The snail's on the thorn:
God's in his heaven—
All's right with the world!
        —Robert Browning, from *Pippa Passes*

# CONTENTS

# Foreword

LIGHT BLOOMS in the morning garden, in globes of tomatoes, ruffs of marigold, rusted daylilies. Light distills into fruit and blossom. Leaves weave fibers of sunlight. And, this morning, after a week of heat and dour rain, I walked out into the garden and found six white roses perched like doves on a bush I thought had mildewed away. And then I found a red rose on a yellow rose bush as though the blossom were flushed with some secret excitement.

I ran upstairs to report, "There's a red rose on the yellow rose bush!"

"My roses," said Bud. "I sprayed them."

It's been so long since we've had a bright morning, one of those artless blue and white skies without menace to cellar or laundry.

Only the marigolds remembered through the dour days, offering wafers of rainbow to affirm the Covenant the clouds obscured. Bees go about their business, witless couriers of the sacred text, delivering crocuses, roses, apples.

But the careful gardener digs a deeper truth.

In the Bible the first law was carved upon stone; affirmation blazed on a desert bush. The seas divided. The sun paused. And the echo of these faraway miracles still sounds in a backyard patch, when you kneel, palm to palm with the earth.

Bud and I live in a big green house that is over a hundred years old with a runaway garden and we have lived here for twenty-two of those years. So the house is full of ghosts of old inhabitants, and the ghosts of our own memories.

I can feel the pressure of time and space; sometimes, very strongly, as though other Americans were coming and saying: "Do it this way . . . remember . . . remember. . . ."

I feel the past very close about me, peering over my shoulder. And I feel the future, because of my children, and my children's children. And I hear the present: some of it dark and foreboding, especially for women.

I hear voices call women to leave the home, to avoid the "trap" of bearing children, to scorn the old crafts and the silent corners of kitchens and gardens. I hear the call to "new frontiers" and the voices are not always pleasing. And then I hear that it is not necessary to be pleasing, or necessary to have a home or a family, that the free woman need not be a mother, that one's true self surfaces best in solitary splendor. I hear about money and what money can buy, about strange freedoms without responsibility and the necessity for anger.

And I wonder about all these things. It hasn't been that way for me.

I hear that the establishment is bad, that America is fat and complacent and indifferent and corrupt and cruel. I hear that in the suburbs we worship money, trade wives, have wild parties, die of boredom, copy our neighbors. I hear that the suburbs are a "female ghetto," that a full-time home-making wife is a slave to her husband, that she is not using her mind.

I have heard that the American people are lazy and mean.

And I wonder about all these things because it hasn't been that way for me. Half-truths are dangerous. I would hate to have a young person grow up to believe that these negatives are the whole story.

I would like to tell a quiet story with many beginnings because, as they say in the song, "Love is a story with no end."

It is a story to listen to when the rain pours down in sheets and splashes off the summer leaves and through the screens, and the curtains sway, and inside there is lamplight and a few familiar heads bent over a book, maybe, or sewing. People still do these things. They do. And the lamplight makes a kind of halo and the rain is an affirmation and the sun, we know, is quietly circling the back of the world and waiting for morning and there is nothing more to do on this day.

So. . . .

Once upon a time . . . there was a family and a home.

And they are there still.

# IN THE BEGINNING

*I am the first of my kind,*
*Oh, the wonder!*

wrote my modest husband Bud, thirty-three years ago. He had dark merry eyes and lots of dark hair, was very thin, not very tall. Why he considered himself so wonderful I don't know, but I believed him. I was nineteen.

He was in the Army Air Force, and the Remington Arms Company was teaching me to sew squares with a sewing machine so that when my security clearance came through, I could be employed operating a secret device similar to Mr. Singer's machine, producing weapons for American soldiers to use in World War II.

It was 1942. Bud was stationed at Warner Robins Air Supply Depot some fifteen miles outside of Macon, Georgia, where we were living—for as long as the Air Force chose to keep him there. We had two rooms: a living area with a bed, a rocker and a chest we had pyramided out of cartons, and an eating area with stove, ice-box, table and two chairs. Water came from the bathroom we shared with other tenants. There was also a sizable platoon of cock-

I

roaches quartered in the house, and I spent a great deal of time dusting table legs with poison to keep the roaches from coming to dinner.

When I wasn't perforating squares at the Remington Arms Training Center, I was typing Bud's poems and sending them to all the magazines we could think of. All the poems came back except one. This was bought for $5 by a mimeographed publication that promptly went out of business. But I still remember the poem. It was about a friend of ours who had been accidentally killed while stationed with troops in Australia. He was trying to teach himself to drive a truck by moonlight in the bush with kangaroos hopping around. Kangaroos, of course, were our idea of Australia. But the idea of a strong young man being *accidentally* killed, when there was so much to be purposefully killed for, struck us as particularly poignant.

All our friends were in the Armed Forces, writing small V-mailgrams describing Reykjavik, Anchorage, London. Our tight little metropolitan hub spoked in all directions. And I, camp-following, found myself staring out of bus windows at the rolling green hills of Pennsylvania, the blue-white flares of open hearth furnaces, that magic triangle where the Ohio, the Monongahela and the Allegheny Rivers meet, the incredibly flat forever of the American prairie, jack-o-lanterns among Hallowe'en corn, and the slow mile-high heave of the land toward Denver.

I love the names of American places. Names talk. The names of the cities in New England say, not only that the people who settled here were from England (New London, New Britain, Cambridge, Exeter), but that those early settlers literally felt they were reliving the Old Testament as they named the towns in their promised land Salem, Canaan, Providence, Carmel, New Haven, Bethel. As you travel west the Indian names begin to unroll their repetitive syllables: Cincinnati, Mississippi, Cheyenne, Walla-Walla. The French stamped La Salle, Detroit, St. Louis, New Orleans, and the Spaniards in the far west marked their language and their faith with San Francisco, San Bernardino, Sacramento. Once I waded in the La Plata River in Colorado and I became a Spanish explorer.

There is a sense of quest that comes with youth. Following Army Air Force travel orders, we charted each new territory for the atlas of memory, computed distances through telescopic eyes and the angle of heartbeat response. We recorded the grain that covers the middle plains and how twin ranges spurt up at each coast so that it seemed a giant might pick up the whole continent by its mountain ranges, one in each hand. Only, if that happened, would the whole country leak out through the silver slit of the Mississippi?

In our summer of '42, Bud was shipped to Jefferson Barracks in St. Louis on the banks of that great river. It was a while before we ever got to see the water, just as, much later in California, it was a while before we got to the Pacific shore, but the sense of frontier was there both times. Once the river marked the boundaries of civilization; beyond lay the wilderness. Watching the waves and the relentless current, you know the water remembers, brings the past right to the shoreline of the present.

We were very poor. Private's pay was fifty dollars a month plus my allotment making a princely total of $80. I got fifty; Bud got thirty. No Equal Rights Amendment then. The government was taking no chances with husbands who might forget to mail their family allotments home. I had holes in my shoes. I remember this because the St. Louis pavement was so burning hot that I had to go to a shoemaker for repairs. But we never thought of poverty. We were self-annointed king and queen of possibilities when we were very young, fighting that long ago war.

I remember sunflowers dazzling on a western wall . . . tow-headed children waving to trains from Oklahoma shanties, those incredible daffodil-headed children protectively colored to escape the crows in a cornfield. Chili, grits, root-beer floats with vanilla ice cream. Some landlady in Texas told me she had night-flowering jasmine and I can still recall the velour folds of summer nights, the strange slow speech, the slurred consonants: "Y' niver tote yer baby, do yer?"

"What?"

"How come y'niver tote yer baby?"

"What?"

"Allus a-wheelin' 'im in thet thar buggy."

Vocabulary and diction were as strange to me as the alien weather: mountain pink and apple blossom snow in February Texas when there would be real snow at home.

Mostly, for me, the war is a memory of wandering freely over this huge land. My land. No, not really mine, not to have, but to share. We were sojourners, not settlers. (I had a neighbor in Texas once who told me she was looking forward to having some *real* neighbors.) We were temporarily stationed, but the land was permanent. I used to watch the freight cars, the ones that said "New York Central," parked at a siding, and I would have a stab of homesickness. I kept a photograph of skyscrapers in a privvy we had in Brownwood, Texas.

People in America establish identities by states, and then by sections of states. Thus Bud and I come from New York

4

State, Westchester County, and the southern end of the city of New Rochelle. But we belong to a greater union as well. We can giant-step, without papers and certifying passports, over one of the largest free expanses in the world. That's what makes us "American."

It has been thirty-three years since we first began our journey, and I feel as though all the old days still walk beside me . . . the changes . . . the excitement . . . the menace of war . . . and the dangers of peace . . . and the abiding joy.

Our private road back to peace was short on cash, but long on children. First Tom came in an Army hospital in Georgia. He was (is) a dark intense boy, full of a firstborn's imperious precocity, quick with questions and answers. When Bill was born, Tom had his question all ready. "I'm going to change the baby," said I one day.

"Good," said he. "What are you going to change him for?"

Bill was fair and quiet-eyed with a gray-green dreamy look like his sister Pam, who came next. And Janet was dark and quick like Tom. All four arrived within eight years. This was the beginning of Bud's career as the world's most unsuccessful ogre. A writer, he felt, had to write in peace and quiet. "I'm trying to work up here!" he would rage at the children. He bellowed exactly like an ogre, but he could always be decoyed by a game: tiddly-winks, billiards, ping-pong, catch, anagrams, charades, even hide 'n seek. And now, all that's left of that fury is the way he advances on all fours toward his grandchildren, growling, scowling, "I'm going to eat you up!" And the child flees, convulsed with laughter, just as our own children fled so many years ago.

For Tom and Bill are grown now, independent, competitive (each tried to reach six feet, each missed by a half inch). They are interested in the things young men care for: active sports, girls, wives, families, homes, enough money to live on a good piece of land. The girls have stayed small and curly haired and interested in girl things: active sports, boys, husbands, families, homes, and a quiet piece of land to live on.

This house, old and quiet and green and brooding, full of windows and growing things, has been home to the six of us and a succession of dogs, cats, squirrels, mice, spiders, an occasional water rat, bumper crops of tomatoes and undependable roses. We fight invasions by maple and mulberry saplings. We celebrate all seasons. We rejoice over the beauty of our old house and fret over a leak we can't locate. We have one car and one television set. And what we have, many Americans have.

So I wonder why this "Establishment" is considered so bad. Can any of our critics explain why we need a wall of law to stem the tide of people wanting *in,* while those countries that are hostile to us need walls of fortification to keep their people from going *out?*

Our streets are still paved with gold. But it is in the form of possibility, not ingots. No mine reveals its treasures without work. It is easy to hold a little country up as a model of this or that perfection. I've traveled enough to know that the American way is not the only way. But there is no other country with a population comparable to ours whose people enjoy the freedom and comforts that we enjoy, and no other country so blessed with good harbors and navigable rivers and forests and fields. We should be proud of our democracy—and thankful for our geography.

To me America is affirmation. YES! A land of unutterable

beauty and variety, and a people who've been trained not to accept blindly, but to cope, to question and to improve.

I could repeat the names of the states like a litany of milestones because they mark the American search for a better home, a further range. Here in New Rochelle, looking out my window I can see the very beach on Long Island Sound where the Huguenots landed in 1688, naming their new settlement for their lost home La Rochelle, which had been sacked by Cardinal Richelieu. They sailed here after the revocation of the Edict of Nantes when Protestant marriages were declared null and void and Protestant chaplains were imprisoned. Here in the wilderness they planted those civilized principles which set America apart from the rest of the world. They declared themselves unequivocally for the inviolable hearth, the sovereign citizen and the accessible God.

But though I exult, as the early Americans did, in the power and variety of America, mostly I love the country because it is home, just as I love my children above all other children because they are mine, and hold my husband above all other men because we made a commitment to each other thirty-three years ago. Out of that commitment has grown the garden of home where it is always seed-time and always weed-time and always harvest.

I'd like to sing the song of a woman whose primary identity was established through love and marriage, certified by motherhood and the no-nonsense hand of necessity, taught and decorated by many gardens.

# "MOTHER, MOTHER, PIN A ROSE ON ME!"

BUD WRITES stories for money. Once upon a time he told them for love. ("The voice of our house," Pamela said later, "was my father telling stories.")

In that magic kingdom the children were heaped like clouds in their Doctor Dentons. They would listen to a bedtime tale by the light of a cookie-shaped moon. Their prayers . . . whssst! . . . straight up . . . special handling. After the ogres, and the wicked witches and the glass hills were overcome, princes and goosegirls always married and lived happily ever after. Our sons and daughters listened to these delightfully "sexist" tales. In those days there was no doubt in their minds that, like their parents, they too would graduate from college, get married and begin Life.

Those were the days before compulsory alternatives.

Tom and Bill and Pam and Janet would clamber over the leaning mulberry tree, or scrunch in the rain-drummed eaves of the attic and discuss their affairs: what treacheries they had suffered from or inflicted upon their friends and/or teachers, what movie to go to, what they would be when they grew up, who would marry first. Tom would naturally do something with numbers. He'd been counting ever since I'd doled out his codliver oil drops: one, two, three. . . . Bill liked to sail, so he'd go to sea. And the girls? Pamela knew she would be a trapeze artist in the circus and Janet thought she'd try that too, and Pamela was in a big sister rage because Janet always wanted to copy everything she did. But in their hearts, they both knew they'd copy their own mother and be mothers too.

And so the summers came and went.

If families have seasons, ours is summer. We have always lived near the water. We all plunge into the Sound madly from the first chill days in April until a few golden leaves float over the face of the waters like dreaming fish. We are all mad for the renewal, the baptismal reaffirmation. And in the summer, during the long vacations from the school year, we celebrate. Therefore, it was only natural that the children should have planned to be married in the summer, in the garden.

Pamela first, because she was the oldest girl and girls had to marry at an earlier age than boys. Bill, according to protocol as second son, should have married last.

But it didn't work that way. We had neglected to consult Micki, the girl who lived down the shore, who had been dating Bill all through high school and college. She wasn't about to wait upon Evslin protocol. Her big sister was already married. In her family, it was her turn. So, the summer of '69, Bill and Mick graduated from the University of Vermont. I remember them in her garden, Mick (out of dungarees for once), dark Indian hair veiled, standing tall and slender as a candle among a cloud of bridesmaids, Bill sunburned and watchful, eyes the color of summer leaves.

Then off they went to medical school in Mexico, car packed with enough wedding presents to set up housekeeping in darkest Africa. We were sure their car would fall over a cliff, that they would be ravaged by bandits or arrested capriciously by the Mexican police. But none of this happened.

Four summers passed quietly, swinging the years around like tugboats pulling the barge of time. Pam and Janet were about to graduate with their nursing degrees. Bill had transferred to the University of Buffalo and was to graduate as a doctor. The school year was coming to its usual close as the May heat blew in a host of pregnant robins and Jenny the cat delivered her spring crop of murdered birds. We set out tomato plants and the willows and maples began the serious business of weaving shade.

One Sunday morning Janet jumped onto our bed. Her face was so bright that I looked down to the finger of her left hand. Nothing there. "TomBurbank asked me to marry him!" she said. (We always called the boy "TomBurbank" as if it were one word to distinguish him from our own Tom.)

Janet has that bright, bright way of shining, as though a 500 watt bulb has been turned on. Her eyes are very dark and her cheeks are ruddy and her teeth even and white. She always looks like Rose Red to me, the bosom friend of Snow White in a fairy tale we used to read together.

"And what did you say?" I asked.

"I said 'yes.' Oh, Mother, I felt so *sure*. You know I didn't know, I've been wondering, but when he asked me . . . so quietly, you know . . . I just had this feeling. . . ."

"You said yes?"

"Yes. Aren't you happy for me? Isn't it wonderful?"

Morning light shone through the familiar white curtains just as if there were no girl on the bed, as if no annunciation had been made. What do you do when confronted by a face full of joy? Do you douse it with prudence? Is this the best boy for her? Will a better come along? Janet is a beautiful girl, has never lived on her own, has a profession where she can meet many people—doctors, you know, eligible doctors.

I hardly know TomBurbank. They've been seeing each other in school and dating for about a year. He's preparing to be a teacher. I respect that. Janet should know what she's doing. I don't. How sure was I when I married? How much was I marrying for the love of Bud and how much for the desire to be married? I was nineteen. In those days girls dated more boys than they do today. There was no reason for me to rush, but I did.

"Deep in your secret heart, pet, do you want to marry him deep in your secret heart? What does it say?"

"Oh, I do, mother. Really I do. He's so kind, so gentle."

What guarantees are there? What can you know? What can an outsider know about the current between two people? I didn't need security when I married, didn't have it. But Janet is different. She wants a nest. And I? What do I want for Janet? For her to build her own happiness as she sees it. She's a wise little girl. *Little* girl? 22? That's maternal mathematics. She's helped me with her good sense over many a quandary. Should I trust her judgment here? Is she too close to the problem? Is she marrying out of fear or love? Or for a pair of sailor-blue eyes?

And what is love anyway? In the mystique I have constructed around my own marriage, I say that I fell in love with Bud at first sight. It is true that our first meeting is still very clear in our memory. But, in all honesty, I know that I met many young men, and the initial encounter seemed propitious, and then, when the relationship petered out, so would the legend I had built about it. I cannot honestly say that Bud is the only person with whom I have fallen in love at first sight. Nor if that first sight was love.

I know that marriage is far too complicated to give more than a hint of its potential during the sense-heightened dance of courtship. You can't play at marriage. The system of trial marriage that many people advocate these days is nothing more than a license to fail. "Why should you stay together when you don't want to?" they ask with the arrogance of ignorance. "Because," I say, "the final commitment, the actual red tape necessary to sever a marriage, provides time for thought." Children stomp out of rooms, hurl blocks at the floor, cry at frustrations. Adults pause and think: what happened? What amends can I make? Marriage is a commitment to the future of a man and a woman and the whole human tribe. It's a commitment that cannot be taken lightly. Yet it comes with a reverse warranty. "For better and for worse" means not only is the merchandise not fault-free, but you promise to keep and cherish it No Matter What. Promises, promises.

Is there one man for each woman? One particular set of soulmates? Do you go around looking for the identifying tag that says: "This man or woman is for you"? Could you read the tag if you found it?

I have often noticed that couples do tend to resemble each other. I don't know if they've assumed the same expression through viewing one another for so long, or if they sensed a certain pleasing affinity from the start.

TomBurbank has the same curly hair that Janet has. He

13

is slender and graceful and quick to smile, as she is. Is this enough? She laughs a great deal when she is with him. I can feel my eyes boring like augers through the ritual of their courtship, and I know that's not fair. I know that one of the greatest crimes a parent can commit is to offer a cold negative response to enthusiasm.

Janet is always in a four-star mood, whether it's up or down. Psychologists may say that this is not a desirable norm, but I don't agree. Bud wrote a poem in which he said, "Nightmares are the penalty for dreams." I think that's true. And I'd rather pay the penalty than forfeit the dream—as long as the emphasis is on the dream, as long as the major mood is joy, and despair is reduced to the position of temporary necessity.

On the other hand, I know it is the responsibility of a parent to counsel and to guide. A blind "yes" can be as destructive as a blind "no." I know that if I try to interfere I may be tampering with a whole life, two lives. Janet may never forgive me. And I may be wrong. Or I may not be able to dissuade and I will only succeed in spoiling the pleasure of these anticipatory months. Or, perhaps it is right to try and stop them; perhaps I will be saving them both from unhappiness.

Bud says he wishes there were still glass hills and trials by ordeal. He wishes he could be a fairy tale king and not give his daughter to any but the bravest of suitors: the one who can kill giants, befriend crones, and balance golden apples. But Bud is not a king, and we have no right to consider our daughter a princess. She too must be fit for ordeal, must participate in the dragon hunt. There are no impregnable palaces, no safe harbors.

And who are we to advocate ease? Did we have an easy

time in our marriage? Were we always kind and supportive to one another? No. Could we have been happier with other mates? We say "No" now because we've come such a long way together. But, in the beginning, before our paths were set, could we have lived happily with other mates? Could we have followed different roads?

Developing one's self is a key value today. Some women say it is bad to go from the protected environment of your father's house to the protection of your husband's. I have been told that my early marriage prevented me from learning how to be an adult!

That statement still amazes me. True, I was financially secure under my father's roof, but I certainly had to forge my own emotional life. Since when is the married state a protected state? You have not only your own problems, but someone else's to cope with, let alone responsibility for a whole flock of children. No, no, I'm not at all sure that independence is more difficult, requires more resources than marriage. By and large, I think the woman at home makes decisions that have greater impact on her small cosmos than any of the memos she may send out from an executive suite "in the world."

Today they say a girl *should* know how to live on her own, to develop more self-confidence before she marries. But, on the other hand, she may find the loneliness so intolerable she will marry anyone. Actually, I think the most constructive reason for a woman to live alone is to realize that singleness is not so blessed. Then, perhaps, when she marries she will be more equipped to handle the hazards; she will know that everything is not gay and swinging "outside."

But no one plans that mechanically. You want what you want, not for one but for a thousand reasons. You can't chart a life with the computer accuracy of a trip to the moon; marriage is a much longer journey really, orbiting immeasurable unknowns. Who can design a foolproof guide for a single human spirit, let alone two people . . . the nest . . . the child . . . the great primal drives?

Marriage is . . . marriage is . . . who knows what marriage is? Made in heaven? Divorce statistics don't speak well for matrimony: more than one in every three unions dissolve! I know a good many divorced people, both in my generation and my children's. It seems to me that those who have remarried are happier, as though they have learned how to choose or how to manage. The ones who are still single don't seem so well off. So maybe the fault lies with the practitioners, not the institution.

But where does all this theory leave my daughter?

Janet sat on my bed, smiling at me in the bright morning sunlight. I could not help but smile back at her. Our whole relationship has been built upon that exchange of tenderness. I took her in my arms and hugged her and felt the soft dark cloud of her hair against my cheek . . . and I wondered . . . and I tried to give her, through my arms, the wisdom to choose and the strength to cope with her choice. Mother's milk confers only a brief immunity.

Later, I went out to my raggle-taggle garden and cut flowers and scrabbled at weeds and pressed my hands to the warm moist earth. Sometimes it is enough just to be gardening, enough just to be out there in touch with the very stuff of creation. Adam's first work was to dress and keep the garden. Sometimes that is enough for the inflammation of ego to subside.

But solving my own problems is easy. I can get hold of them. I know the parameters of possibility. I can handle consequences—at least thus far. My children's problems are something else again. And especially when those problems are mixed with strangers and that whole dark web of currents that spin around the hub of sex. "Tell me, God, what shall I do about my daughter's wedding? What can I do? What should I do?"

You have to bend your head in the garden—to find secret fruits and hidden enemies. And sometimes, when it is warm and the sun is bright, a vertigo comes, the same as must have stricken the Greek oracles when they came out of their caves and stood in the bright sun to prophesy.

I kept my hands to the earth, my fingers playing with a purposeful idleness about the weeds, as if I were a pianist, practicing. And then the words came as they always do when I ask. "*Now,*" the Voice of the garden said . . . and I thought if I looked up I would see the Gardener, and I knew I would never look up. But my fossicking fingers picked up the message.

"*Now,*" I heard. "There is only *Now.* *If* and *Maybe* wait behind every corner, hatchets poised, daring travelers. But, if the boy and the girl truly want to stand here in this garden, you must tell them to make each *Now* as beautiful as possible."

"But," I said, "how about those kids who are so interested in the pleasures of the moment that they let their whole future slip by? Is this what you are advising for my girl?"

"No! That blank stupor of drugs, of chemical happiness, is a denial of natural aptitudes, of intelligence, of perceptiveness and active response. Tell your daughter and her boy to take each moment and *value* it, not to wish for another day, another time. But take today and if it thunders, exult in the thunder, if the house tumbles, exult in the strength to rebuild, and if the sun shines and flowers bloom, pick the flowers and give thanks. You must learn to be happy today, if you expect to be happy tomorrow. It takes wit, eyes, heart, will and love. Love makes its own luck."

Two squirrels raced across the high wire of the maple tree to our rain gutters where they did a bit of housekeeping.

A dove wept.

I repeated the words to myself, delicately packing soil around a tilted cosmos, shaking dirt off the roots of wild intruder grass. I felt the long afternoon wind like a cloak around my throat and bare shoulders. The yard darkened as the sun dipped. Only the two lawn chairs that Bud and I have placed to watch the evening come, only those two chairs remained in a pool of gold.

"Tell them that is my wedding gift, the gift of *Now. Now* is life. Tell them to use it well."

I knelt and heard the flowers chime their customary carillon: "Give. Bloom. Be. Spend. Don't go broody to seed. Cut us while we're fresh. Keep using our bloom and we will keep blooming. Emotional thrift silts the stream. . . ."

I don't pretend to be Joan of Arc. I don't think I have angels in residence. But even the most rigid materialists believe ideas "come." From where? Can they say?

I remembered a line about casting your bread on the

waters, a tale of a miracle where five loaves and two fishes fed a multitude.

So, I thought, if it is Janet's desire to give herself to this boy, I must have faith in her choice. There is no easy road to human relationships. Ease itself can be a snag. Man was born to trouble; but sparks kindle light.

"Now!" said the dandelions, throwing their yellow caps in the air. "Now!" said the hydrangea, sending out blue runners in search of the sun so that in one overgrown corner of my garden I have a shaft of sunlight where the hydrangea have literally stretched and rooted themselves. "Now," said the grass briskly, getting to work.

In spring the earth busies itself with the anonymous sheathed possibilities of winter, sowing flowers, flowers everywhere. Can we do less? Can we be of such little faith?

# WATER-WATCHING

AS A PROFESSOR of American Literature, I teach Thoreau, of course—and I think about him sometimes.

Thoreau went to the woods to live by himself and find out what life was all about. He built his house and hoed his beans and paddled in Walden Pond at night, playing echo tag with a loon. And since then, a host of other literary solitaries have headed for the woods in search of primal truths and spiritual communion. There must be a great deal of splendor to a private universe, to be a solitary witness to the intimate business of the earth, removed from the world's demands, chatter, pollutants. Sometime, before I die, I suppose I'll have a chance to try this monk's robe . . . but while my bridegroom is still around, I prefer more sociable celebrations.

"What did this guy Thoreau have against the world?" asked one of my more perceptive students, an adult "retread" (one who goes to school part-time to catch up on missed college). "Why was Thoreau so down on everything?"

"I don't know for sure. But his girl refused to marry him. He didn't have much money. He didn't enjoy working in the family pencil factory. . . ."

"Didn't he ever marry? Take care of a family?"

"No." Teaching becomes exciting when students challenge from their own life experience.

"Then how could he know what life was all about?"

"He said to simplify."

"Simplify! He simplified all right, all by himself. You know he didn't like it. He just stayed at Walden long enough to write a book and then he came trotting back to town."

My student may have been correct. Thoreau, that most famous hermit, was always going over to the Emersons'. When he was alone, he was chattering away to the world he despised, writing book after book, hoping someone would listen. The world wasn't too interested.

Echo Bay on Long Island Sound is our pond. We don't have to flee to it. It's right down the block, a part of our lives, and our best times together. When they were four years old, each of our children learned to swim there, making the final triumphant journey from beach to float (without a life-preserver), sputtering, arms and legs churning like tiny paddle wheels. They learned to jump from terrifyingly high rocks at the water's edge, to play water tag, to swim under water and emerge in secret places under the float. They honed their muscles through the fluid disciplines of weightlessness, achieving competencies in the strange watery environment that gave them more poise on land.

In grade school you could always spot our water-based children in gym classes. And you could always tell new residents of our neighborhood from the old; new children would be a little city shy or strident until sun and water literally laved them into belonging. Here children work along with their parents to keep the boathouse clean, to get the floats in and out of the water in season, to paint and caulk their own boats. And when the cement pilings were eroding away and the whole boathouse threatened to fall into the Sound and the masonry estimates were outrageous, the whole neighborhood turned out. Mothers and fathers and children, directed by neighborhood architects and craftsmen, proceeded to mix mortar and repair timbers. The estimate was $13,000. We did the work for $300. And the gains were far more than financial. Perhaps one can take to the woods and get away from the world to find some higher communion. But the solitary's truth is only a fraction of the whole.

God, watching Adam in the world's most beautiful garden, knew that he was lonely and sent him a companion. "It is not good for man to live alone," He said.

I agree. But then I am a family person. I can swim the hundred yards across our bay and lie on our rock alone and wait till the weather is warm enough for my hero, who does not have my tolerance for cold water. But the morning that I hear Bud chugging behind me and see him clamber ashore, dripping like some great bearded sea monster, my simple rock becomes a throne I gladly share. Summer is officially begun. And I know a year has elapsed because he breaks the ailanthus branches that have grown to block the sun.

In summer we play "spook" out on our rock. Spook is a game of mental anagrams. One person starts with a three letter word, then each player adds a letter in turn: *t-o-e* becomes *r-o-t-e,* then perhaps *t-o-w-e-r* or *o-r-a-t-e* and so on.

The player who can make no more changes receives an "S." The first one to miss five words has become *S-P-O-O-K.* He loses.

We lie out on the rocks, amphibian, at home in land and sea. Sometimes a jolly tugboat pushes a barge of sand up channel to the cement company. Then all the children on our float yell: "Blow your horn!" And the tugboat blows its horn, and the black dog who rides the tugboat wags his tail, and all the children shriek in an ecstasy of pure noise.

Sometimes a motorboat comes exploring. The masts of our neighbors' sunfish unfurl striped banners. And, if the wind is right, the white-winged schooners fly, pirouette, drop sail decorously and go to bed. That's what the captains say: "Wanna help me put my boat to bed?" Lines coil like sleeping snakes, hatches battened: they're good housekeepers, our sailing neighbors.

Once, when the children were small, we had an old boat. The sail kept ripping. I had to patch it with all the rag-tag of my dress-making materials. I remember crouching on the floorboards and pulling the jib-sheets, my mouth dry with terror. Those were the days when Bud had to show what a good sailor he was. The local paper (desperate for news in those days when the town was small and uneventful) would pick up stories from the Harbor Police blotter and often report: "Family with four children and dog towed home under ripped sail" or "Family with four children and dog towed home with smashed rudder." The neighbors smiled discreetly and Bud would not be pleased.

But now that we're old enough to stop pretending, and those of our children who want sailboats have their own, Bud and I have settled for a canoe. We glide around islands where sunken boats sleep and tall grasses grow and mother ducks come to teach ducklings to heel. Herring gulls roost on Chimney Island and on every old piling that rises at low tide the herring gulls perch like weather cocks pointing into the wind. Sometimes a spray of silver signals flying fish and the gulls will scream and pursue. They say gulls fly over rocks, a clam or mussel clenched in their beaks. When the gulls attain sufficient height, they hurl the shell with bomb-sight accuracy so that it breaks open on the rock. Then they swoop down for appetizers: clams on the half-shell, mussels in brine. I've never seen this, but I've seen the litter of shells and bird-droppings on the rocks.

Our Echo Bay is a way station for Canadian geese, long-necked, white-tie, formal birds. They glide among the squat mallards whose iridescent heads mirror the water's shine. We often canoe past a cotillion of dancing birds, ducks sashaying with geese around some invisible maypole. Gulls rarely deign to swim. They may bob around like toy buoys, but when they've any place to go, they're in too much of a hurry. They take off, wheeling, screaming, mocking, and the geese may follow, barking like dogs.

One March when Pamela and I came down in our divers' suits to beat the season, a whole cloud of gulls came and circled our heads. In our rubber helmets we must have looked like delicious fish. I remember Pam's eyes, wide and gray as the sea, as she said, "Look! So many gulls! They made such a shadow I had to look up."

We were adrift in the firmament, gull-shadowed, but the fact that we were together, that she could say, "Look, Ma, look," and I could respond and share her wonder, doubled the miracle.

The swans are our greatest sea treasures. I always thought a swan was a royal bird, reserved for illustrations in children's books. But we have our private family of swans. Bud brings them bread and they come to the float and beg like dogs. Then one day we were in the water, just Bud and I; it was middle tide and supper time and most of our neighbors must have been inside. The pair of swans with their four cygnets were swimming around the low tide area we reserve for children. Mother Swan had her neck in that swoon-beautiful angle buried under her fluffed up wing: "preening," I like to call it; picking her lice, ornithologists say. Three of her cygnets were already white, but the fourth was still dark and he was always off by his wild lone I noticed. Shy? Adventurous? Who knows what makes the deviant?

That day the dark one was on the beach exploring. Bud and I were noodling quietly in the water when suddenly Father Swan came bearing down on us. He stormed up to Bud and beat his wings and extended his neck in a posture we had often observed when he wanted to drive interloping birds away. Swans are supposed to be voiceless, but "keck-keck-keck-keck" said Father Swan, unmistakably. And I'm sure that message would not bear polite translation.

Bud was frightened. They say a swan's bill can bite through a man's iron work-shoe, that his neck is strong as a whip, his feet like hammers. Poor Bud was no match for Father Swan on his own territory. This was my moment. You see the swan wasn't looking at me. This was my only moment of bravery in a long life of fear of heights, of lightning, of automobiles, footsteps, shadows, speed—you name it. Daredevil I am not. But this swan was a menace to my love—sounds corny, but it's true. I was not frightened. I was furious. I turned on my back and kicked up a storm. "You go 'way, you!" I said in my best school teacher wrath. "You go 'way right now!" He did.

I met him later, swimming alone as I swam alone to my rock. He cruised very close, turned around to watch me land, and I watched him haughtily all the while. "You're only a bird," I glared. "You mind your place." He did.

Early in summer, before the cygnets hatch and the families split away, we counted thirty-five swans, coming at our canoe from all corners of the bay like a corps de ballet. But they were just dreaming about their business. I think the belligerent swan was either trying to divert us from his children or he was angry at Bud for not coming with the customary bread. Mostly, they dance slowly in and out among the low tide islands,—slant, enigmatic eyes, proud heads, grace incarnate.

I remember an afternoon when Bud took Janet out in the canoe. "Let's paddle in the path of the sun," she said, and he did. They followed that golden wake past the sleeping boats . . . tide sinking and rocks blooming like Disney slow motion photography. And then they heard that unmistakable propeller throb.

A swan skated across the surface of the water, awkward, wing tips like rapid crutches beating the water, mighty legs and neck stretched taut. Exactly like an airplane working up enough speed to become airborne, his wings beat great flaps in the air, and then the noise subsided as he glided away.

"That's a real gift," said Janet, "to see a swan fly."

It is. But I know a greater gift. To have a daughter who shares this feeling, a young woman whose mature perceptions have enhanced, not blunted her child's sense of wonder, who can feast with us on water and wafers of sunlight, who swims, as all our children swim, with such long clean strokes that we can always identify our special school of fish.

Poor Thoreau, he had only three stools in his hut. He never wanted more than two guests at a time. He had only a pheasant for companionship, and the pheasant really cared more for her chicks. We can cut wood as he did, smell fresh peppery resins. But we do not sit by our fire alone. In our game of Spook, "heart" makes "hearth" as "h" is added. Is this "h" for "home"? I look it up in the Etymological Dictionary. They give the Icelandic *hyrr* meaning ember or hearth, no root for heart, no connection between the two words. That's the knowledge you lose if a book is your only place of information. We, who know the heart, know the real source of hearth.

What I mean to say is that in summer Bud and I and our children (and the dog in the early morning before the bathers come) play in the water together. We know the warm surface and the cool eddies, black stormwind and beaded sunlight. Sometimes we swim at night and the phosphorous particles in the water cloak our strokes with an unearthly radiance. The summer moon is red as a watermelon. It drowns, drowns, drowns, new moons always coming and drowning near our quiet rocks.

We know the magic lessons of the water. To a casual observer, it may seem the wind is just scribbling quick graffiti on the waves. But look again. The same hand that wrote "Mene Mene Tekel" in letters of fire, wrote chapter and verse for the sea. He teaches the perils of rage as the dark scowl of a puff sweeps across the water and suddenly, predictably, rocks our boat. Water sings a hymn to instant response where Light is absorbed and celebrated with diamonds. We learn the quiet method of examining everything: not blankly as mirror, but transforming an angle, adding a radiance, undulating the reflection of a rigid rock as though water itself were a presage of mortality and reincarnation. The Spirit smiles scrutably on the face of the deep, mixing a liquid compound of sky to remind mortals who forget to look up.

Water is our last frontier, our final wilderness. The shape of the Sound has not changed since the last glacier. Indians paddled here as we do. Some primitive man may have stumbled out of his cave, been stymied in his progress by the water, and made up some story to explain it. Water affirms a world in which we are not the Particular, but just a particle.

We speak of the mysteries of "The Deep" that confound the imagination . . . before the heavens were separated from the earth and the sun was hung in the darkness of the firmament. Then God said, "Let the waters bring forth abundantly the moving creature that hath life." And the sea teemed with strange experiments in life and motion. Shall a skeleton be an outside shelter like the mollusk, welded armor like the lobster, or an internal spine like the fish? Creep, crawl, float, fly . . . ? Prowl. Walk! In the beginning how the Artist must have experimented with His theme! Science tells us that the salt content of the blood is the same as the salt content of the sea. As if it were the salt and not the spirit that has made us cousin to the restless, questing, repetitive, changeable sea whose nature is so closely patterned to our own.

We don't need a book to affirm what our senses apprehend. We don't need solitude to recognize the presence of eternity. I prefer the horizon carved by the bulky silhouette of my husband as he sits in the bow of our canoe. Sure, I can lie on a rock and commune with my soul—no question.

Water soothes and renews. But I'd rather share my communion with my mate.

Philosophers ask if a falling tree makes a sound if there is no one around to hear it. I would like to put the question one step further. Is a sunset beautiful if no one watches? And further—if we watch alone, if we cannot turn to someone else and say, "Look, isn't that beautiful?", if we cannot see our own response doubled in another's eyes, is that sunset less for us?

Yes, Thoreau, man is sociable. He has a great need to show and tell. Even the visionaries seem to come back to their desks, seem to be impelled to share their ideas with the world. Fine. Fine. But the world is made of strangers. Some may listen; some will not. To share an experience *at the moment it occurs* with someone you love, to know that from that moment on there is one more bond between you, makes the fine careless rapture of today a pool from which you may both drink during the inevitable drought of tomorrow. Seeing, and loving, and being, and belonging fill the cup.

The family, of course, goes even further. What we have loved ourselves, we have shared with our children. We pass on this gift of inheritance without the penalty of death, as they will pass it on to their children, and their children's children. For the paradoxical mathematics-defying reality of love is—the more you give, the more you have.

Water-logged, sun-struck, moon-devouring, we commune with nature . . . and with each other . . . as the Evidence confirms the message. We are not alone.

*God setteth the solitary in families.*

# WEDDINGS AND ALTERNATIVES

SO WE PLANNED for an August wedding and set about sprucing the old house.

What accumulations of dust did I find, moving books and couches for the painters! I once read a book about a lady recently moved to Maine who said her new neighbors came and checked for dust behind her picture frames. I'd never pass that one.

We were all busy pulling weeds, pruning bushes, catching crabgrass. I had to buy material for Janet's gown, and for Pam's, who would be Maid of Honor. That was fun, weighing bolts of white for a wear-it-once-and-put-away dress, finding a caterer, planning a menu. Arrangements, arrangements—one gets so caught up in an assembly line of events that there is no turning back. And do you want to?

"Bud and Dorothy Evslin cordially invite you to attend the wedding." No, change that. We want our guests to do more than *attend*. "Bud and Dorothy Evslin cordially invite you to celebrate the wedding of our daughter Janet to Thomas Gibson Burbank." Janet lettered the invitations carefully in brown ink and they looked much better, we thought, than the traditional cold printed cards.

The day before the wedding it rained so heavily the

caterer couldn't put his supplies in the cellar, and I had to send Pam and Janet downstairs to bail. I had just painted the cellar floor red and the cat was making bloody pawprints everywhere. After all the bailing I went downstairs and the rooms were flooded again and I scolded the girls and then I noticed that a small spring had opened up under the cellar door. The leak was so situated that to fix it you had to keep the door open and allow more rain to pour in.

I bought this Masonry Stop-Leak that swears it will stop Niagara. It didn't. Bud and Pam crouched down there quietly, talking, pressing gobs of cement against the oozing floor. I think they both had qualms, felt overwhelmed by circumstance, were relieved to be making drip castles on this strange beach as if the action recalled the many hours when play was their most important bond and the Future was no fiercer than the next wave.

Twenty-two years we had lived in this house and never had such a flood. Then I realized that Janet in her zeal had pulled up all the weeds that were near the house, and these weeds had probably acted as cistern. What would we do if it rained on the wedding day? Could our house hold a hundred guests? No. And Janet still had to buy shoes and I was waiting for the shoes so that I could hem her dress and Pamela developed a swollen eye and she called Bill—our emergency long-distance doctor—who assured her, in his quiet healing way, that it was just a bee sting and would probably subside. It did.

After a heavy rain the sun spins ropes of crystal. Everything sparkles, wind-scoured, sun-dried. Leaves catch flat paillettes of light and toss them to one another. Butterflies flicker among the roses. Apples swell. The golden trumpets of my neighbor's squash have climbed the fence to herald the wedding.

And, of course, the best thing about any celebration is that it brings the whole family together. Tom and Bill came home, and as I walked off the porch into our garden, walked on the arm of a strange young man, there stood both my sons with cameras. For a shutter's second they looked at me; forever I will cherish that moment of walking towards them in the garden, seeing them similar, definitely brothers, straight and busy and serious as young trees.

Mick, Bill's wife, was pregnant and she wore a red dress. The color and her own happiness accentuated her shape in that graceful way that a woman's body has of becoming more beautiful when it carries an odd load—like a Polynesian with a basket of fruit on her head—not bending but becoming more supple, more erect under pressure. And Darlene, the girl our Tom was soon to marry, sat apart a little, observing her new family. And then it was Pamela's turn to come down the path. My pearl-cheeked Snow White looked lovely in her sprigged muslin and wide pink hat, but her gray eyes were shadowed. I could feel the snake in her heart whisper, "Older sister, spinster sister," as though she were that much older, or anyone cared. Or was it only the hissing of my overwrought imagination?

Caterer's men poised on the flower borders. Rows of strangers sat in our yard. And then the record changed. "Here comes the bride . . ." on Bud's arm. Bud, like Old King Cole, merry brown eyes crinkled yet solemn, white beard tilted skyward, had a warm sturdy arm for a girl. "Here comes the bride." Rose Red all in white, head bent (how vulnerable a bride looks in her angel costume!), took that swift definitive walk on a summer Saturday to the altar under the mulberry tree, their play-tree, where a new game would be sanctified. "Here comes the bride . . . Here comes the bride. . . ." Pamela standing tilted forward slightly, Bud waiting, handing his girl over to her young man, the spectators discreetly amused. "Here comes the bride . . . Here comes the bride. . . ." The boy who was working the record player did not have a very good view of the procession and was not that interested. He played and played the record until the end.

And the next morning our neighbor's daughter Sarah came and sat on our front stoop and watched the birds peck the rice off the walk. She kept her eye on every sparrow. It was Sarah's first wedding.

Slowly the house came back to earth. Grass began to grow beside the table where the food had been spread. We finished eating the leftovers.

We harvested fresh corn and string beans and the tender green onions pushed their bulbs out of the soil and said, "Pick me. I'm ready. Pick me."

There is a time to sow, and a time to reap.

Janet and TomBurbank set up housekeeping in a duplex in Ossining with a tiny balcony, really only big enough for tomato plants. But Ossining is not far from the college where I teach, and I could scoot up occasionally and have lunch sitting hunched on a tree stump we'd scrounged from some lumber yard. We'd picnic and talk married woman talk and there would be a glint of Hudson River down the block, just as there's always been a glint of water from our home. Janet made me toast and grapefruit and eggs delicately fried in butter, and I admired her plants and her wedding presents and watched her face and we told joys and troubles to each other as we always had.

And Bud went apartment hunting with Pam in Manhattan. What she lacked in domesticity, she would have in glamour. Okay. Rule #1: heads up. Bud walked around the hot summer city, steered her past neighborhoods where he didn't want her to *walk,* let alone *live,* and finally brought her down to Jane Street, a quiet brownstoned block in the West Village where the shutters are neatly painted and doors have bright brass knockers and vines climb trellises and children play stickball in the street and, if you did not happen to notice a sign saying: "This street is patrolled at all times," you would have no idea that anything more sinister than than a lover's tryst ever occurred here.

Everyone who wants to live in the city has to solve the primal equation: Shall rent equal *space* or shall rent equal *safety?* Safety means a doorman and an intercom from the lobby and free bi-weekly extermination service. Bud persuaded Pam to opt for safety, fourteen stories up in a new building. It was really the thirteenth floor, but the most hard-headed New Yorkers get suspicious about "13," and landlords, who are equally hard-headed, simply skip the number as they label floors. Her apartment had clean white walls and a great corner window with an elegant view of the stone geometries of the city under a blue stenciled sky. She had one room and a tiny kitchen and a laundry in the basement that was off-limits after 10 P.M. This cost $250 a month, a bit more than her weekly salary, but not impossible.

She had found a job as medical editor for a big publishing firm, using her nursing degree, her academic background, and her charm. I am "in publishing," she could say. Being an editor placed her firmly at the top of the New York mystique, much better than being "just a nurse." Living alone is the great adventure. She was young, healthy, with a good job, living in one of the nicer parts of Fun City. She most certainly was not "stuck in the suburbs;" she was no one's chattel, no one's slave. No dirty diapers to change, no one to please or clean up after or feed.

The trouble with me, I've been told, is that I cannot believe anyone can be happy who does not live as I live. I am told I must respect different life styles. I try to. I've just never known a happy woman living alone, or a happy man, for that matter. Of course, marriage is no automatic ticket to happiness either. Nothing is. But it helps, I think.

On the other hand, viewing a girl's success only by her marital state is an insult. Pam was barely 24. She had the whole world in front of her. How about that "Now" I considered so important for Janet? Doesn't it operate for Pamela as well? "Now" is not only for couples. Happiness, I think, comes first to the perceptive, to those who really *see* where they are.

Pam moved in finally, dropping a box of crockery in sheer exasperation as she carried it to the car. Janet and her husband Tom helped, and we helped, and probably Pam couldn't wait to get rid of us, because the adventure would not finally begin until she had shut the door firmly upon us and upon everything that was so dusty with familiarity, until she could discover by starlight the new walls and new shadows that would belong only to her.

At home her window had been no higher than trees. Here she would float above roofs, moon high. Traffic would honk from faraway canyons like the geese in Echo Bay. I imagined the elevator clanging shut, and footsteps down the carpeted hall, the night song of her air-conditioner like a city cricket.

So, on that hot summer night, we left our daughter locked securely in her tower. But, unlike cruel fairy-tale parents, we hoped some prince would find his way to her door. We knew that in all good stories, beauty always triumphs over wicked enchantments. But we knew that, in life, all stories are not good.


And soon we had another party to go to. That's the thing about big families—little time to brood. Tom (our son Tom) was to marry Darlene. As the mother of the groom, the details of the wedding did not occupy me. We could be just guests. And again—celebration—the whole family together. Janet, newly married, brought her new set of parents as well . . . we grow, we grow! Pam had a young man from whom she soon danced away. Micki, bigger than ever, the child still biding its time. And my two sons, officiating this time, being photographed instead of being the photographers. They stood dark and straight in their rented finery, stiff white shirt fronts. They stood together waiting for the bride, their heads inclined toward each other like young penguins. Darlene was late. Tom was edgy, dark eyes smouldering; Bill, experienced, counselling cool.

And then Darlene came, in a lovely cream-colored crepe. I could feel Tom relax—just a trifle—the ceremony was still ahead. And I watched Darlene's eyes dart around the assembled company. The child is frightened, I thought, very frightened. . . . "No, she had contact lenses on," Tom told me later. "She doesn't like them."

The old question: will she make him happy? Note, of

course, the mother's bias. Again, I didn't know Darlene well. Tom has been away from home for a long time. He met her when she was a student in a computer course he was teaching. Their story is that she raised her hand the first day in class and asked him, "How far do you go?" And he answered, "As far as I can."

"What do you think, Bud?" I said. "Is she the girl for him?"

"How do I know? I've known Tom all his life . . . listened, identified. (I remember, I remember, the low sound of their voices in the living room deep into the night, Bud on the couch, Tom pulled up in a chair, their matching furrowed brows, Tom's speech swifter than Bud's, less sure. I would hear snatches of baseball, numbers, politics, and later, the sheer abstractions that were to shape Tom's professional future.) How can I give a fair answer?" Bud said.

But I am a teacher, a professional evaluator of strangers. "Can't you be objective?" I said.

"Absolutely not."

So Darlene became an Evslin and there was a lot of dancing at the wedding and she danced very beautifully, and we danced and Tom danced and Janet's new family danced too.

And that summer of celebrations became memory.

# PEACE IN YOUR HANDS

SO OUR HOUSE finally emptied. No children left.

The boys had been going for years: Tom at fourteen to Andover and on to Harvard and straight out to the world; Bill at seventeen to the Merchant Marine, the University of Vermont, medical school, marriage and the world. But Pam and Janet were more dilettantish about their education, and I suppose we're partly to blame here.

I dropped out of college myself to get married. I was scrawling boys' names in the margins of my textbooks and the only dates I was interested in occurred on Saturday nights. As a teacher and retread, I know that the woman who goes back when she's ready (I was forty, my homework finished) is a pleasure to teach and a fabulous learner. Older students test much higher than their younger colleagues. So I didn't press my daughters. They went away to school. They went to work. They traveled. They came back and each decided to go into nursing which seemed a fine practical decision to us.

Of course, feminists say: "How come your son is a doctor and your daughters are *only* nurses?" And I have to say that nurses are equally important, that my daughters would rather heal by touch than by text, that they did not choose to spend years in medical school. They wanted to marry and have children and allow the burden for financial support to rest primarily with their husbands. So, at this point, the feminists and I agree not to lunch together.

Every morning, during their years at Pace College, Pam and Janet drove off in their Dutch Cleanser nurse-in-training costumes. Aprons and white stockings danced on my clothesline. The girls pored over heavy books, dissected the necessary cats, and applied deft bandages to Bud, who loves to be nursed. But, like everything else in families, this period passed.

Our house was really emptied. And it's a rather big house. However, if you've lived in your own home for over twenty years it means: (a) in terms of today's prices, you have a fantastic bargain; (b) every room, every shadow, holds a king's ransom of memories; (c) every room, every shadow holds so much absolutely essential debris that moving becomes an unthinkable operation; and (d) if you didn't have the spare bedrooms, no one could sleep over and that would make uncomfortable visits for emigré children.

So, of course, we wouldn't think of moving.

Bud and I walked around the empty rooms, went to work and came back, got dinner together and cleaned up. There was a kind of pleasant newlywed peace to the arrangement. When we were first married, before Bud went into the Army, we lived in furnished rooms. Before he was discharged, we had Tom . . . and then everyone else arrived. So that actually we'd had very few nights alone in our own house—never a long stretch.

But suddenly, it hit me as if I'd come up against a wall. It's over. The girls are gone. That's it. That part is finished. I don't fancy myself a possessive mother. I know everyone has to do his or her thing. If my daughters were still living at home, ages 22 and 24, I would certainly be concerned. I know what my own nest means to me, and I want no less for them.

But, as I walked down the hall one September Saturday the sun was shining with such intensity on Janet's pillow that it seemed as though the sun were searching for her too. The untousled room was preternaturally still. I could feel their pet names, "Pamielle" and "Janetu," dry on my tongue. Nothing to straighten out and put away; no chores to do or nag over.

Freedom loses its charm when it means no one to curl up and say those quiet things that mothers and daughters say to one another: not only the "he said" and "she said" of normal gossip, but the fascinating "I feel" and, more mundane, "With my green top, what skirt shall I wear?" The world does not necessarily shake with these confessions, but, for a long time, they have kept me on an even keel. Focusing on other people makes life more interesting, less selfishly intense. Now our mother-daughter chats were dependent upon the logistics of time and space, transportation, and differing commitments to the world.

I walked past my daughters' empty room to the little sewing room that was once a nursery and once Janet's room when she was older and the girls decided each wanted a room of her own (after they had tried it for a year, they got lonely and came back together again).

The sewing room is the only room in the house that is not a corner. It has two narrow windows and juts a bit from the front of the house, right in the middle, like a busybody afraid to miss anything. Many, many years, all those years at home. . . . Memory buzzes around this sewing machine:

slipcovers, girls' dresses, matching the slipcovers out of remnants (till Bud said you couldn't tell where the small girl ended and the big chair began), dolls' clothes, my clothes, patches, repair, disguise, re-cycling, zig-zag, buttonholes, the outlandish embroideries of bobbin and spool, double needle stitching . . . what have you. The quiet hum of the sewing machine, the drift of fabric through the presser foot, the cool pins, up, down, up, down, round the spool and round the bobbin—this has been my tiny orchestra. Deep into the nights, one problem or another faded because no abstraction could survive the concentration necessary to cut correctly and seam straight.

Now I had a problem again. Not a real problem. That is, nothing soluble, but one I must learn to live with. The sewing machine waited, patient as a good steed, tethered to the table as if the girls were still home, as if it had not just made a wedding dress and a maid of honor's dress, as if it didn't know the difference between such cosmic creations and sewing six pillow cases out of a sheet.

For two dollars I had bought a bag of leather scraps. Red, green, brown bits of leather tumbled out of the bag, and then, like a jackpot, a whole gray skin with white markings —a gray deer? Just about the size of a deer. What to do with this trove? Ah! I would make clothes for my missing daughters: a skirt for Pam out of the gray because her eyes are gray, a patchwork jacket like a coat of many colors for Janet who is brown-eyed and ruddy cheeked. I love to feel fabric. I'd never worked in leather, but this was very soft. The pieces fluttered in my lap like the colors of approaching autumn. I felt like Mother Nature making a collection of recollections, the way trees, when they lose their protective green, flower again with whatever color they can summon up, quilting the roadway.

My mind could float, thinking about the girls I was making the gifts for. I could imagine them wearing these garments; it would be a type of hug from me to them. Crafts and creation are fine for their own sake, but when you can imagine a beloved face smiling and receiving, your pleasure as creator is enhanced. It's great to do your own thing, to fulfill yourself. But it's even greater when you're not doing it for yourself.

And it's also fun.

I cut a jacket pattern out of purple jersey from my remnant drawer, and then set to work, cutting the leather into triangles, placing them patchwork fashion on the pattern pieces so that the two sides of the jacket would balance like a squared quilt. Then it was easy to sew the leather triangles to the jersey. But it took a long time. And that was the special joy of it. Mindless, yet concentrating, my fingers had to twist the little shapes under the pressure foot, had to sew a neat edge, keep the scraps flat, no lining showing; up and down went the needle, up and down the rust and green aisles. And I discovered as I sewed, what I knew I would discover: pleasure in the gift and peace in my hands.

There is something about hands, touch, my fingers on the leather really manipulating the fabric of love. "Touch wood," we say for luck, as though a magical circuit initiated by our hand upon wood must deliver us from evil. The soldier fingers his medal or his lucky stone or his girl's picture. Why? When all else fails, why do we turn to touch? Why should blind physical contact be comforting? Are we looking for something long lost? Do we hope to get "in touch" again?

The climate of the womb is warm, fluid. The newborn, blur-visioned, frightened by empty space, cries. We pick it up, pat it, and it quiets, soothed by touch. Space is intolerably new, but a hand is warm as memory. The infant responds immediately, enters the human community through the touch of his mother's breast, cheek, encircling arms and deft fingers. Before the sophistication of sight and hearing, comes the elemental cognition of touch.

When we meet, we shake hands. When we love, we embrace. When we hate, we strike. Touch is the language of our deepest emotions; so, when we sympathize, we say we are "touched," we "feel" for somebody.

Christ, revealing himself in the garden, warned the Magdalen away. He said, "Do not touch me." He was not ready. The affirmation by touch was reserved for a greater day yet to come.

In life, as we know it on earth, touch is primal. The living regenerative impulses toward light, toward water, dark, air, are all touch-oriented. Cells go where it "feels" good. And it came to pass in time that the rays of light touching primitive retinal machinery produced sight. Sound waves hammered the delicate anvil of the eardrum and broke the primordial silence. Thus each sense is created by the pressure of a specific impulse upon a particularly constructed receiver. It is all touch, all variations of response to impact.

Perhaps that is why pure touch, one human being upon another, is so meaningful, why the great ceremonies of baptism, marriage and death are solemnized by touch. Perhaps touch stirs some private memory fledged before the corruption of thought, when each stimulus was meaningful, when to live meant simply to respond. Before clothing and shelter became our shabby substitutes for Eden, before the tool and the weapon, we used our naked hands. Now progress has gloved our souls. We flick a switch. Hands off! Man is more than otter or antelope or gull. He is capable of more than gross motor responses. The skeleton of a man's hand, as Thoreau noted, is not so different from the vein pattern of a maple leaf or the webbed pad of a duck. But in man the bones are freed from the casing. The thumb is opposable. And with his manual aptitudes and his cranial convolutions, the responsibility for salvation and/or damnation was thrust firmly into man's hands. That hand can murder or create.

The caprice of wind and time scribbles elaborate patterns in tree and sand and stone. But man is more than a receiver or a blind sensualist. Created in God's image, he too wants to create. Some theologians and poets have pictured God as sculptor, shaping Adam from a handful of clay, carving a rib named Eve into the first scrimshaw. Or as Michaelangelo painted it: God reached out his hand and touched Adam and lo! there was life.

Hassle subsides. "If" and "Maybe" and "He said" and "She said," taboo and despair and pain all retreat before our native wizardry: the in/out of a needle, the deep foraging of a trowel. Hands provide an extension of private realities, a patio of occupation wherein the busy crafter rests, renews himself, taps some vital intimate circuit. It is as if one were poulticing one's own problems through the laying on of one's own hands.

Indeed, it seems to me that crafts are really TM (Tran-

45

scendental Meditation) American style. Restless as we are, imbued, perhaps subconsciously with Franklin's "The Devil makes mischief for idle hands," with the Protestant work ethic that insists we do something (even if that something is only watching TV), it may be difficult for an American to sink into a Nirvana-producing meditative trance as the Indian gurus prescribe. But it is easy to meditate when you're doing something, to be your own guru. Let's call it PM, Productive Meditation.

In hospitals they call it "OT," Occupational Therapy, cure by doing. It has been observed that a patient eases his concentration upon his wounds simply by doing. Creativity awakens a new sense of self; a more competent, less vulnerable person emerges, one who has met the challenge of material and left his mark. A picture grows on an empty canvas. Someone smiles. A line of color stretches meaningfully through planned space. Metamorphosed material expresses the artist, surprises the viewer.

Possibilities are infinite. A pile of beads or seeds, hanks of wool, a blank wall, a loom strung like a harp awaiting the music of the weaver, wooden mixing spoons and simmering broths, paper, tin, clay, sand, silk, snow . . . everything waits, secret, pregnant with promise. All alone, without the aid of group or funds, a person can perform the miracle of hands.

Fingers are friends, always ready to serve, to build, to divert. When we are very earnest, when we want something very badly, it seems natural to clasp our hands in prayer. Perhaps craft is another kind of prayer. Maybe we want to get back to the image from which we were fashioned, to create, to use our fingers, whose dexterous versatility puts all tools to shame.

"That's all right for some people. But I'm just not creative. I could no more paint a picture than I could. . . ." Neither can I, but I can follow a pattern. All masterpieces are not museum caliber. Perhaps the current vogue for crafts expresses our deep need to break through the prefabricated barriers we have erected. Perhaps labor-saving is not always the wisest economy. Maybe our intense goal-preoccupation has denied us the pleasure of process. Perhaps the greatest "bargain" is some fragment of beauty we can create for ourselves.

The restorer of old furniture, the needlepointer, the gourmet cook find satisfaction not only in the end product but in the intricacies of method. And, if someone asks later, "Where did you get that table? pillow? casserole?" it is rewarding to answer, "I made it myself."

Macramé, quilting and rug-hooking may have been the creations of Yankee thrift, but they mend frayed nerves as well as frayed budgets. I learned to sew during the war when Bud was overseas and I was too upset to read. "Peace," said the needle as I jogged down the seam. "Peace, peace," said my fingers, smoothing the fabric over the metal throat of the machine. I made a red skirt, I remember, and that red cloth caught the light and filled the room and absorbed all my attention.

So, once more in a time of unease I found myself in my sewing room. I made my daughters a skirt and a jacket and a hat and a bag all out of those two dollars worth of leather scraps and some salvaged jersey and zippers. And suddenly I realized: this is my "Studio." Why not? Is it not filled exclusively with the tools of my trade: swatches and lengths of fabric, a palette of threads, pattern library, sewing machine easel and ironing board frame? Am I not creating? If I am not actually *making* money (that militant participle seems to validate activity in the eyes of official feminists), I am certainly *saving* money which—considering taxes and inflation—comes to the same thing. I am happy in my studio. I am concentrating. I please both myself and my loved ones.

Next time someone asks me what I *do,* I think I'll say I'm an artist or in "fashion design." That ought to impress. I can easily show my studio. My work? "All sold," I'll say. That sounds important. "All my masterpieces are walking around or tacked to furniture." Just a housewife indeed! All those years in my studio I was creating canvases, one still life after another, to decorate my dearly beloved customers. And everything sold like hotcakes.

# DOES A TREE HAVE BUSINESS WITH THE SKY?

BUT LIFE is not all home, or the memories of home.

There is a time to plant and a time to pluck up what has been planted. Since my own crop is harvested, I try to keep my ties with youth and to use what I've learned by sharing my love for the English language with my students. This has become my "work."

Teaching, some say derisively, has always been woman's work. But if you are proud of woman's work, if you love the challenge of young minds, then teaching becomes a natural extension of a working life. My students are a new family. I know it. And they know it too.

So, come fall, I report to school, meet my suntanned crop of students, pencils sharpened, eyes bright with good intentions. I can feel their muscles ache with the loss of summer's freedoms, hear the rust clank on the old thinking machines, see the boys size up the girls and the girls size up the boys and the more adventurous choose seats side by side.

They all size up the teacher. "What will she want of us?" "Can I give it?" "Can I fake it?" I watch them: the raised heads, the lowered heads, the fidgeters, the listeners, the hand-wavers, the irrepressible commentators, the window dreamers . . . all variations upon the theme of response. This is the ever-changing repetitive fabric of my working hours. It demands total response, requires my full attention. While I'm in front of that class, they're all I know, all I need to know. Ask any teacher.

There is no discipline problem. I teach in college. But Westchester is a community college. We offer a second chance: open enrollment. Any Westchester resident is eligible. Most of our students are blue collar, on the way up. They cannot afford to mock the establishment; they want in. But they are not used to expressing abstract ideas. Many of them have never read one whole book! Indeed they judge assignments in inverse order to the number of pages. Many of them go to college full-time and work forty hours a week in filling stations and supermarkets. Sometimes they fall asleep at their desks. "I'm not good in English," they say. "I've always hated it." Sometimes they say they no longer hate it. For starters, I just try to get them to see, and to say what they've seen.

This October, according to the newspapers, the sugar maples are holding their leaves too long. The newspapers say it means a severe winter when the trees don't drop their leaves, when squirrels store extra nuts, when sheep grow thicker coats.

Every day a new show plays along the road.

I tell my students to watch it. I say, "Write a composition about what you see on the way to school."

"I see cars," they write.

"I see the white line."

"I see other cars with crazy drivers."

"I see policemen hiding in speed traps."

"I see red lights. I count to eighteen and they change. I step on the gas and my engine coughs."

"I see a long empty road. I can't resist it. I go 90 and the policeman around the bend says he knows I was goin' 90 because he heard me comin'."

"What did you *see?*" I insist. "What did you *see* along the road this fine October day?"

They have that blank earnest look that falls over a class like a cloud when they try to answer a question that just does not make sense. They are result-oriented. They like to oblige.

Finally—a hand: "Trees."

"Yeah! TREES!"

So they know they've seen trees.

I can see their trees, lollipop shaped and indistinguishable as the cloud across their faces. A blur of trees as they drive along the highways.

Harassed, bewildered by my nonsequiturs, they are still trying to please. I am reminded of Job's questions: "Wilt Thou break a driven leaf? And wilt Thou pursue the dry stubble?" It is not my role to test them with inscrutable trials. I try to simplify. I must bring them to some new frontier of perception—or I have failed as a teacher.

"How about the sky?" I say. "Has anyone seen the sky?"

But of course they are not like Job. They were not remotely crushed. They are a good normal self-esteeming American class.

They laugh. At me. Warmly. We are in it together.

"Whaddayu drive, Proffesuh? Was you drivin' that green Mustang this mawnin'? You bettuh look where you're dri-

vin', Professuh. Neveh mind all them trees, that sky stuff."
Then school is over for the day.

Six o'clock October traffic creeps around the winding
Hutchinson River Parkway. No accident stalls this traffic.
The sun, like a bright hand, presses against each windshield.
No visor helps. Dazzled cars edge over the hills, sun splat-
ting windshields, blotting the road. I inch forward—into
the valley of light—before dark.

One tree, too soon stripped, scratches the sky.

What waits behind November?

Leaves, summer rich, still fur the trees. Here and there,
like an immolating dervish a maple burns and whirls—
blood red, flame gold, tangerine. Purple vines fetter patient
trunks, chaining beech and oak to earth. I see the branches
rise in horror; webbed, crepitated fingers of oak snap at
wind, flee the encircling purple vines.

Leaves fold gold, hold light like Chinese lanterns, illuminate the winding road, dance light. But only a few do.
Something waits behind November. The ailanthus drop
brown-paper-bag leaves, mulberries shrivel. The sumac is
purple and dour, quiet.

Every day as I drive to work I watch the show.

Stiff leaves tack down in slants of wind, square rigged,
flattened on wind currents. You would think a leaf would
arrow to earth. The old lake makes a watercolor blur of
shore. Willows hold grimly to their green witch wigs, strip-
ping, growing yellow at the root, a reverse bleach. Privet
still beaded, still green; five tattered poplars, spinster slim;
darkness waits in the wings. I can feel November black
against my throat.

Tuesday's flaming sugar maple is charred and dead by
Thursday. A bright yellow tractor, iron child of yellow

leaves, toddles wide-legged down the road. A stray red maple in war paint whoops it up beside a frazzled birch. Wind puckers the lake. Ducks hide in the shallows, still and puzzled, like rocks. I try to read the illuminated scrawl of the dying year, to cull some meaning from the gaudy signature. "I AM THAT I AM," said the bush to Moses in the long ago desert fire. Am what? What do You mean by *that*, I AM? Is *that* the Difference? Are You the emblazoning of the unique? Are You trying to tell us that in the end, in the November of our lives, we must make a public reckoning? In spring, You say, trees have just begun to be. In summer they blur in a green daze of fertility. But by November, to illuminate the darkening road (for new passengers), each tree—the slow, the swift—distills a private memory of sunlight—gold or crimson, spire or Catherine wheel—and those trees who have forgotten all light curl up in brown despair. So people, perhaps, in their November, are marked by the light they remember. Some shine, and some do not.

Motorists, brooding over steering wheels, are caught by separate splendors: a tall sycamore with vines demure around its ankles, stork-legged elms, a cluster of beech trunks wrestling like pythons. Color blots against the sky, flares in a few separate candletips. What does it mean, I Am, this final violence of the year? Is it Rage, I Am? Is it War or Celebration, Defiance or Victory? When You write with letters of flame, what do You mean?

Does a tree have business with the sky?

Branches reach, dipped in light. Do they seek a sustenance against the coming dark? Provide. Provide. Funnel the final sunlight to the dark bark. "Give it to me." "No! Give it to me!" Reaching for light in a final mad struggle, bleeding scarlet and then clotted dark, leaves slash their fingers against the smashed blue glass sky.

So the webbed hands of the trees will hide no more nests, strum no more wind song, cup no more light, play no further games of shadow on the grass. They are betrayed, finally, by the musical wind who, as I watch horrified, snaps each leaf stem and sends the little fellows, still eager, still furious, about some further business. "Take me! Take meeee!" They shriek and snap and race after the fierce gusts of cold.

"F-R-E-E-E-E—" they sing. I can hear them as they skitter foolishly across the road. "We're F-R-E-Eeeeee! You're dead, oh tree. Oh stupid, earthbound clumsy tree. Look at meee!"

"No! Look at meeee!"

The day snaps November as clouds of leaves skitter from branch to branch, run across the road, spatter our windshields, settle for a moment in the gutter, and then snatch up again, mad, still wind-dry, buoyant. "Oh no, let's cross the road! It's better on the other side." A whole flock of silly leaves races across the road, swirls in figure eights, half-gainers, do-si-do, ring-a-levio. It doesn't matter. They lose. They sink disconsolately against the sodden earth to warm the nests of old beetles and sleeping roots.

The autumn tree says many things about a time to burn, and a time to sleep, the folly of flight and a greater wisdom that even has a purpose for folly. The wheel of the year runs down the river road to the sea where all endings begin. And we motorists will drive in the dark for a while.

In school I listen to the pens of my students sighing over their papers. What did I see on the way to school this morning? What did I see? Five golden trees, four calling cops, three horns a-honking, two stalled cars and a Professuh . . . who asks too much of me.

One girl wrote: "On my way to school every morning I have to pass a lake and I like to see this lake. It makes me feel good."

I was glad to have her in my class.

# DAUGHTERS

PAMELA'S RIDE to work was decorated by the autumnal colors of the graffiti scrawled all over the subway cars. Passengers choked on and off. "Let 'em off! Let 'em off!" howled the conductor. Elbows, feet, chins, pocketbooks, briefcases—one reacts less to persons than to parts of people stuffing themselves through the rubber-lipped sliding doors. Wheels screamed at the track. End car doors slid shut, did not latch, then gaped open foolishly as the train lurched.

"Sure, Mom," she said wryly as we met for lunch one Saturday afternoon (me, as usual, half awed and half fearful at the enormity of a girl living alone in New York these days), "publishing's fine. We're doing a book on Wound Drainage Systems."

And then we had one of those wordless conversations that you have with a person you know very well, who wants you to know certain things, but doesn't want to say them right out. We were eating in one of those health food restaurants in the West Village where they specialize in home-made soup and fresh baked bread and clean tumblers of spring water and lots of plants hanging in macramé nets

—a nice place. We talked lightly of this and that, but the picture I got was this:

Yes, she knew wound drainage was important. After all, she was a nurse, but as a research project it was something less than exciting. Arriving at the office she would hang up her coat and notice that everyone else was already at work, and that certain powerful eyebrows were lowered disapprovingly. She also knew that she had survived her three-month probationary period and it would be difficult to fire her. "G'Morning," she'd say (I can just hear that soft don't-care voice that had infuriated so many teachers).

Once she swore she would never work or live where she could not look out a window. Now she was doing just that. If her boss called, she could go into his office and see the gray elephant flank of the Empire State Building. They count prestige in New York offices by windows. And by how thick your carpet is and whether you have a couch. Couches rate very high on the office totem pole. Some day, if she was very lucky, she might have a window and a carpet and a couch too. And maybe even someone to bring her a cup of instant coffee. Odd, how office advancement is marked by these commonplace comforts of home.

Re-order, reprint, illustrate, bind, type-face—the words smell of new ink and reamed paper and great presses rolling and quiet libraries, oak and dark. Books and stories were the sound of her childhood. She had always loved them. She had wished for books, for a good job, for independence. But you must always beware of fairies who too lightly grant wishes. There is always one qualification and they never tell you what it is.

"Pam," I said. "By the end of November you should be due for a vacation. Why don't you take a week and visit

Billy and Mick, get out of the city for awhile?"

She smiled. I could already see the wind in her hair. "You know, I might do just that." The leaves of the hanging plants stirred as we left; the city sun was slipping behind tall buildings, shadowing the street.

Our son-the-doctor Bill lives on an island. That's another thing I love about our children. They're always one up on us. We love land and water and have a little of each. But Tom bought a Vermont mountainside with a waterfall. Bill has a house on a Casco Bay island, a ferry ride from Maine Medical Center in Portland where he works.

And don't think I didn't go to the hospital, flying in the first time I came to visit. Bill had said, "Meet me at the hospital and I'll take you out to the island." So, I went, dutiful and delighted, arrived at the reception desk and had the operator page Dr. Evslin. "Who shall I say is asking for him?" she said. And I said, "His mother." (What else could I say, or would I want to say for that matter? It *is* great to know that your son can heal people.) So he came down— white doctor wings, grave smile—"Mother, I don't believe you said that!" And it became a hospital joke, that I asked for my son the doctor, that all through the hospital on every vestpocket intercom the message beeped: "Billy's mother wants him. Billy's mother wants him."

Anyway, Mick and Bill have this house with a round windowed captain's room and a view of the winking lights of the bay and a sun parlor where Micki has made slipcovers with bright poppies on them and the sun, like a giant poppy, plops behind the Portland skyline. We've clambered with them down a vertical embankment (over which the house will undoubtedly plummet if they don't check the erosion). We've walked along their low tide beach and collected shells and what Bud calls "remarkable examples of perfectly ordinary stones."

And all this would be perfectly splendid if Micki were not about to have a baby. When they took the house it was summer and there were many ferries for the summer people. But winter on a dour Maine bay is something else. First the ferry lines went on strike. Only two boats a day sailed. Bill had to sleep at the hospital, leaving Micki home alone. "Don't worry," Bill said. "The fireboat comes for emergencies." But the fireboat was moored on the mainland and would have to make the trip out first. Then the fireboat broke down. We thought of making a deal with a lobster fisherman, but that didn't seem quite the thing to do.

So, as we'd decided, Pam, who had a week off and was a trained nurse, went to stay with Micki that last week in November when the child was due. Now Mick is a city girl. She was brought up here in New Rochelle, in a house with a garden, but if she ever went outside it was shopping or to the theater. She's not a nature buff like us. Those long winter nights when the wind blew off the bay right through her little sunporch, rattling the panes of the captain's room, waiting for Bill to come home after those 36 and 72 hour shifts that interns serve, stuck out on an island without a movie, with few young people (Even the lady next door, whom we were counting on, moved to the mainland for the winter.) and Bill coming home often tired, upset, not up to her eager greeting: these are the conditions divorce feeds on. The pill for instant happiness doesn't always work. Up rage and freedom; down patience and love.

She had two dogs: Osa, almost a German Shepherd, and Murphy, a cross between a Labrador and a horse, who quietly tunneled right through the basement and out into the yard, just to help the erosion along. When things were quiet, Murphy could always be counted on to chew a pillow; he adored polyurethane.

But Micki loved being pregnant. She is a tall, very slender girl. She put on extra weight that she needed, carried the child competently. She had the sturdy look of a tree that for some reason may have a bulge in its trunk but grows on happily, waving its arms, taking on its leaves. And the only sign she may have given that she was fearful was that she allowed the giant dogs to sleep on the bed with her when Bill slept at the Hospital.

So Pam's visit must have been a comfort. They lived in totally different worlds: Pam in the heart of the bustling city, "free," but menaced by population; Micki "stuck on an island," tied to her family, menaced by solitude. I have an idea each envied the other. They were so different: Pam small and dreamy, Mick tall and swift; Pam with her medical competencies, Micki with her physical needs.

It rained heavily in Maine that November. The sunporch was too cold to use. The girls huddled close to the fireplace. The house winked with the copper and colored glass and bright straw of Bill's years in Mexican medical school where they had begun their marriage. You know a home partly by its accumulations, the history and geography of acquisition, where the purchasers were, what they cared for. Like Mick and Bill, the little house on the island is jolly, bright-eyed, deft-fingered.

Pamela's Manhattan room was high and glassy above the teeming city, confronting the naked geometries of stars. Mick's house was wood-panelled like a ship, moored close to other houses, buffeted like an ark by wind and water. Indeed they were planning to call the child Noah. Of course

61

it would be a boy, and then they could say they lived in Noah's ark and Bill's marine and biblical fantasies would both be certified at once.

"Do you think it will come tonight?" said Mick, shivering, moving closer to the fire.

"Nah," said Pam, wise with her two weeks on maternity service. "First babies never come on time."

They went to bed and the rain stippled the Bay and Bill called in as he always did to see if everything was okay. And Osa and Murphy curled themselves up on the big bed and the two girls went to sleep. The baby moved during the night and woke Micki up, but this was usual. She snuggled closer to the warm bodies of the dogs and went back to sleep.

And in the morning she called Pam into the room and showed her how the bed was wet.

"Wow," said Pam competently, "Your waters have broken." They phoned Bill. They phoned the obstetrician. Because of the ferry schedule they couldn't wait around too long. Take the 10:30 or wait till 3:00.

They packed Mick's suitcase. Packing a suitcase for a first baby—that is something to remember. You're packing clothes for a mystery: arms you've never seen, eyes that have never seen before. The essence of newness will be swaddled in these quiet jerseys. You pack fear into the suitcase too, unutterable fears get folded into corners. You know there will be pain, but you pray that labor will be your only pain.

The two girls, related not by blood but by love, marched up the ramp onto the waiting ferry. Pam offered to carry Micki's suitcase; Micki refused. Pam preferred to ride outside, to let the spray pearl her lashes and cool her cheeks. But they went below decks, because Micki hates cold. They huddled together on the smooth wood benches. The vibrations of the engine set up little eddies the child could feel. Suddenly Mick was suffocated with laughter. She hid her head in her hands and her shoulders rocked.

"Oh, Pamela!" she sputtered finally. "What if it wasn't my waters breaking at all. What if it was one of the dogs?"

"Wha-at?"

"How could I ever tell them? I'd be so ashamed."

"They'll know," said Pam comfortingly. "They have ways of testing these things." After all Pam had had two weeks on the maternity floor.

The foghorn of the ferry brays like the lonely ghost of a crazy donkey as it glides into Portland harbor. They debarked among the damp rope and pilings of the dock, past the six ancient men who wait on the pier forever like emigré customs officials for a regime long overthrown.

Bill met them at the admitting desk. He was trying to keep his medical cool under the first-father flush, trying to remember what he and Mick had learned together in the Lamaze natural childbirth clinic, the things he was supposed to do and say to his wife to ease her travail.

"Ah, yes, your waters broke," said the obstetrician and he did the test for waters breaking and it came back positive. "How often are your pains?"

"No pains." Micki has these wide brown eyes, the kind Tom and Janet have. They get very solemn in the presence of serious questions. So the doctor proceeded to induce the birth and the birth did not want to be induced, and Micki, who is extraordinarily narrow-hipped and not fond of pain, began to regret the whole affair. Bill walked around in circles and Mick was at that stage of the delivery when the Lamaze says you don't want anyone to touch you, not even your husband. And Bill touched, "There, there, Mick," he said, "just relax," as the course had told him to say, and she said, "Go 'way, Bill, don't touch me," just as the course had predicted she would.

So Bill went out of the labor room and there was Pam and she pursuaded him to come outside with her. Brother and sister took a turn together around the windy streets of Portland and invoked some old twinship they'd always claimed for each other, being the two green-eyed members of a brown-eyed family, being the closest (only twenty months apart).

They had spooky affinities, like having a toothache at the same time, mispronouncing words in outlandish ways which became doubly ludicrous when they started on medical tongue twisters. They share this way of tuning in and tuning out whereas Tom and Janet, the brown-eyed quick ones, tend to live more in the present tense.

Anyhow, Pam made Bill eat a dinner of sorts in the hospital cafeteria, and the other nurses and doctors said warm joking things. And I know how Pam wanted a baby of her own, but I'm sure she never said so. Later they went back upstairs and there was Micki, having a perfectly ghastly time. And it became apparent to the obstetrician that his test was inaccurate, that Micki's water had not broken, that the puddle may, indeed, have been caused by an incontinent dog. And, because he was a good obstetrician and Bill's friend and colleague, he felt terrible. He stood by Mick's bed and gave her everything he could think of to ease her pain.

They began to monitor her heart and the baby's heart and

Bill, who understood the necessity and the implications, had to stand by and watch this girl he loved—as husband, and as doctor. It was his wild nature lust that urged this city girl to live on an island where logistics had probably contributed to her decision to rush to the hospital. Perhaps the baby was not ready. Perhaps it was weeks too soon. Maybe the baby . . . maybe the baby . . . maybe Micki. . . . I can imagine what he imagined.

And then it was all over.

No boy was born. The ark did not get its Noah. But there was a little girl the color of apricot with dark sleepy eyes and the perfect number of fingers, toes, dimples, lungs, eyes. The pediatrician checked the baby carefully and Micki forgot all her pain. She beamed at her new tiny princess, happy as a queen. And they phoned us at home that midnight. Tanya weighed in at six pounds eight ounces. Everyone was well.

*A woman when she is in travail hath sorrow, because her hour is come; but as soon as she is delivered of the child, she remembereth no more the anguish, for joy that a man is born into the world* (John 16:21).

And joy in the birth of a girl as well!

Bill marched all around the hospital where his friends were working and he said (and Bill is the quiet type usually), "Have you seen my daughter? Have you seen my daughter? Pretty cute, eh? Pretty cute."

Pamela phoned and her voice was soft. "She has such bee-yootiful skin," she crooned, "such soft, glowing beautiful skin. . . ." My heart ached for Pamela's loneliness even as I exulted and welcomed our new girl.

# BIRTH AND ALTERNATIVES

BIRTH BRINGS beginnings of deep emotions, of long range plans. Today the subject of birth has also ushered in NON, the Association for Non-Parents, and the new freedom of alternatives that everyone is advocating these days. Down with the sexual stereotypes! Down with the old life styles! Free women from the hassles and humdrum of childbirth. Never mind that most jobs are tedious nine-to-five bores. A job pays, and, according to Betty Friedan in *The Feminine Mystique,* "money is the only status a commercial society can accept."

"Change" has become the word for today; "Establishment" and "stereotype" the evils of yesterday. New cars, new homes, new fashions, new life styles glitter. Conditioned, perhaps, by advertisers and by greed, women are urged to rush to the new without a thought for the value of old traditions.

But—without mothers, the world simply stops. When a girl is told that she is lowering herself by becoming a mother, that motherhood is no-account drudge work, replaceable by day care center and uneducated cleaning woman, that girl is told to deny the splendor of her own anatomy. The woman who patterns her life style after a man's rejects her own unique heritage.

And who are the chief spokeswomen for this role changing? Simone de Beauvoir, Germaine Greer, Gloria Steinem —one a life-long mistress, one married a month or two, one never married. Kate Millet, married but with admitted lesbian tendencies. Betty Friedan, divorced. What can these women know about marriage and children?

How can a girl who has never had a child know what she is rejecting? "Stereotype" means to fix in a permanent form. The stereotyped woman, if you ask a feminist, centers her life around home, family and sex. The further implication is pejorative: these activities are mindless, a homemaker does not use her "education," a woman would be better off if she dropped her Victorian fetters and went out into the world and acted exactly like a man. Who wants to be *"just* a housewife"?

I've read many articles about the new life styles where married women (they haven't been able to quash marriage yet, but they're working on it) are driving pick-up trucks instead of picking up their children. Women can be telephone *linepersons* (liberated: strapped to a pole). According to the *Guidelines for Equal Treatment of the Sexes in McGraw-Hill Book Company Publications:* "Instructional material should never imply that all women have a mother instinct or that the emotional life of a family suffers because a woman works. . . . Do not say 'Henry Harris is a shrewd lawyer and his wife Ann is a striking brunette' because women's physical appearance should not be described unless it is also described for men. . . . Women in a grocery store should be called 'customers' not 'housewives!' " I think it strange that there should be any guidelines for non-fiction beside the truth. And I wonder why the mother instinct, female beauty and home-making are suddenly taboo. Because they're stereotypes?

But *stereo* means *solid* in Greek, a fixed, solid type. And we are forgetting Who stereotyped women. Freud said anatomy is destiny; the feminists claim that anatomy is NOT destiny. Certainly, with the new freedom of the three C's: cars, can openers and contraceptives, a woman need no longer be a full-time mother and housekeeper forever. Motherhood need not be chronic; as a matter of fact the chances of cure are very high. But to deny a woman her anatomy is another matter!

Aldous Huxley in his *Brave New World* envisaged the test-tube babies. "Mother" and "Love," he predicted, would be scorned words, and his women received a "Pregnancy Surrogate" pill when they got edgy, because he knew the female constitution demands the fulfillment of a child. His is the book that in the early thirties predicted television, the drug scene, automation, supersonic travel, genetic control, disposable everything, licensed promiscuity. He was amazingly perceptive about the condition of women as well.

I have met lovely young professional women, married, bright, the kind of women who should be having children like themselves. And they have said to me solemnly, their voices soft, their clothes chic (that much of womanhood they do not renounce), "Oh no, I don't want to have a child. Neither does my husband. If I had to stay home, I'd climb the walls. I don't want to be tied down." They accept the confinements of an office; why do they wince at the confinements of home? Because motherhood in some classes of society has gone out of fashion, that's the dreadful, simple truth.

An amusing thing happened at a women's studies seminar I attended. One of the panelists who was advocating wider horizons for women disappeared from the discussion for about an hour or two. When she came back, she was breathless. "My son has just won the national college wrestling championship!" And then she burst into tears. "You're right, Mrs. Evslin. You're so right. Nothing is as important as your family . . ." The militants in the audience were shocked. But the new alternatives for women suddenly became less significant.

"A lovely girl like you should have a child," I have said.

"Why? Because I'm pretty?" As though beauty were irrelevant.

"No, because you're a fine young woman and the world needs people like you."

She was somewhat mollified, but still, "I want to have a career!" Her voice was shrill, reminding me of the leaves skittering off the October trees, those leaves who think a tree is just an old stick in the mud.

"Have your career," I said. "By all means have your career. But have your family first. Life is long. You don't want to be *just* a careerist all your life. There's time enough for everything."

"No, No! I want my career now."

"But it's better to have your children while you're young. For your health and that of the child, it's better. And then you can live long enough to enjoy your grandchildren as well."

"Oh!" Face alight with comprehension. "That's what you're after! You're just like my mother. You have the grandmother syndrome!"

Indeed I do. That's what makes the world go round.

During the war we lived in a succession of cross-country furnished rooms, far from family and friends, never knowing when Bud would be shipped overseas. We never would have planned for a baby under those circumstances. But thank God, we are not the sole architects of our destiny. It seemed to me that I was a girl, then suddenly moonshaped, and then there was always a child attached as though I had become suddenly part carriage like a maternal variant of a centaur.

But this was fulfillment, female fulfillment. I had suddenly, beautifully,—flowered, become a functioning member of the greater cosmic harmony. I was obeying God's commandment to living things. And even now, when I go out into the garden and look at the flowers, it seems to me that God speaks in roses and daisies and thistles. And His Word is "Life!" And then more life. As e.e.cummings puts it: "to the poking, prurient fingers of the scientists/ the earth answers with only/ spring."

When a woman gives birth, it is more than a flight record for some cross-pollinating bee. When a married woman gives birth she sets the particular seal of immortality upon the uniqueness of her love. The strange vined dance of the chromosomes confirms the roots of two families. Under the antiseptic white lights of the delivery room, in a strange posture, out of love and pain, a miracle is born.

We speak of "getting in touch" with the great basic rhythms, of responding to natural forces. Then, for the survival of the world, a woman *must* fulfill her stereotype, must exercise *all* her options, her uniquely female ones as well as the more mundane abilities she shares with the rest of the world. Motherhood is a beginning, not an end. It opens horizons, illuminates corridors. And, of course, it is not always heavenly. This is earth.

But Tanya was born and Bud went up to the little house on Peak's Island to help Micki after her mother had left. Bud freelances; I am controlled by my job. So Bud went alone to greet the baby and he phoned and he said, "She's beautiful, so beautiful." His voice was more excited than it had ever been with our own children. Perhaps the years have taught him—now that we are the parents of such fine young men and women—the years have taught him what as a young father he did not know: the infinite possibilities in a sleeping child, the smiles, the ideas, the acrobatics, the skills, the torments. "She's already a person!" he exulted. "When she cried I held her very tight and she loved that."

And then he called about midnight. He was babysitting. Mick and Bill were out. "What shall I do?" he wailed. "Her navel's coming off. How shall I caulk her?"

I remember that in New Rochelle that night there was a great ice storm and in the morning all the trees were sheathed in diamonds. School was cancelled. I walked the dog around our quiet street. I was having a taste of living alone, not only the children gone, but Bud too. I thought of our little new family, the bright patchwork nursery that Mick had made with calico windowshades and a garden of pillows. There was Bud learning to be an English sheepdog nurse like Nana in *Peter Pan*. So my house may have been quiet, but I was certainly not alone. My roots had sprouted in many places and all the plants were connected.

I went into the house to take advantage of the day off, to

catch up on papers. I enjoy this simple professional life. But I am only a way-station in the lives of my students, a memory soon dim. And to me, too, their changing stream of faces is fixed only briefly, then flows away like cloud shapes. But to Bud, to my children and my children's children, my true identity is confirmed. Perhaps they are more important to me, in some ways, than I am to them now that our relationships are on an adult, voluntary basis. The mathematics is not important. But I know my "true self." I have lifetime tenure. I will never be a mother emeritus.

As Nietsche said: "Out of chaos comes a dancing star." And Shakespeare: "These present woes will serve as sweet discourse in times to come." And God said: "Be fruitful and multiply and replenish the earth." And this is the way my world has turned. Now into the third generation. And I look at it, and I see that it is good.

How I wish some of those beautiful bright-eyed young women would turn a deaf ear to those who, in the guise of opening alternatives, really close them. Every rule has exceptions, of course. Some women are not made for motherhood. But God did not make "persons." He made Man, and he made Woman, stereotyped, fixed. Rage is too simple and scapegoats only surrogates for problem-solving. Marriage and parenthood are not easy, but abdication is not a mature solution. Only fairy tales end: "And so they were married and lived happily ever after." The rest of the story is for adults only. But it's a great book, all the pages empty . . . waiting to be filled.

In our family Bible three marriages and one birth have been inscribed. I feel as though for these three new families, the music has begun. Only my own girl remained in the wings. Pam, who once wanted to be an aerialist in the circus, lives high above the city in her eyrie of glass and steel. She tosses her curls and protests that she loves her freedom. She's adopted an old white cat someone left in the trash. He sheds all over her blue studio couch. But he greets her. He will not eat when she's not there.

Sometimes, when things are not all smooth between Bud and me, or when I sense some misunderstanding between my children and their mates, I think Pam is the fortunate one because she does not have to compromise, because she is free to do her own thing. But I know this is not true. Because loneliness is not her thing.

# HANG SILVER BELLS!

DARKNESS COMES early in December. I drive past a forest of witches' abandoned brooms leaning against the late afternoon sky. The days are getting shorter so swiftly, you can almost feel the top of the globe slipping away from the sun. Sometimes it seems we are coming into a place of eternal darkness, and I remember a story I read somewhere:

One day toward the end of June, God said to Adam: "Believe in me, or I will take away the light forever."

And Adam, who in this tale was created at the end of December so that he knew only lengthening days, said, "Nonsense. You can't take the light away. As a matter of fact, I've noticed that each day is a bit longer than the one before it. You'll have a hard time taking the light away. You'll be bucking the trend."

But this was Midsummer's Eve, the 21st of June.

God decided he would teach Adam a lesson.

At first Adam pretended not to notice. Then he said, "Oh, it's just a storm threatening." But no storm came. So he began frantically to clear away the trees that were casting such offensively long shadows. And God stripped the leaves from the trees so Adam had nothing to hide behind. The light was leaving the world. The power of darkness grew.

"Now will you believe?" God asked.

Adam was frightened, but he was also very stubborn. He pretended not to listen. And God said no more. With his hand He just maintained a gentle pressure on the globe so that it tilted a little more each day, and finally, on December 21, Adam saw the red sun slash into the flesh of the sky and it was still afternoon, but the whole sky bled. . . .

"Oh, my God," he said, "the sun is dying. The sun is bleeding all over the sky. I can't live without light, Lord. I can't see where I am. Help me. Help me!"

And God said, "Do you believe, Adam?"

And Adam knelt and bowed his head away from the terrible darkness. "I believe."

Gently, so as not to topple the trees or disturb the rivers, God released the pressure of his hand. Day advanced and night retreated. Sunlight summoned the leaves out of hiding. And the fullness of light was restored to the world.

But, every year, towards the end of June, there's a pause in the great spring bloom. The sun slowly retreats, silent and unmistakable as the lengthening shadows. The descendants of Adam remember, and believe.

I am a great lover of the sun, and terrified of driving on dark nights. I always relive Adam's fear come December when I have to drive home at five o'clock and the sky leaves the road pitch dark.

But I've noticed one interesting thing about the winter tree-scape that flanks my path. Although the frail deciduous trees have been stripped by cold, the brave conifers remain, as though God did not want to remove all green magic from the earth. Lost in the verdure of summer, you never see a spruce or fir or a pine. But in December you can see how isosceles proud they stand, how green furred and elegant among their scrawny neighbors. Is He saying, in one more way, that brightness flashes on and off while the quiet ones endure? Or is He saying there are many ways to be?

But man is a gaudy creature, flower-prone. Perhaps we are grateful to the fir tree for its color under cold. It seems to be the guardian of life. So we hang glass apples and cold silver bells, winter blooms, to remind the earth of spring. We wish to tilt the globe once more toward the sun.

As I drive home along the winding river road, I think I would like to decorate that hemlock, the one that stands alone, spiked against the evening star. And then, when the sun comes back, when the pattern of withdrawal has been reversed—even though our coldest month is yet to come— we know that the Light has been returned. It is only natural to kindle our festooned trees and celebrate a Birth.

# OLD SONGS

BUD AND I believe in snow and fresh air. When I was a child my mother always said, "Go out in the fresh air." My children complain that I said the same when they'd come weeping to the kitchen door, noses and fingers snapping off from frostbite. And now, come January, when I have a month off, Bud and I take four days, go to a ski lodge and overeat. After the four days we've generally had it because the tariff is rather steep and because nights in a communal lounge and combination bed-sitting room can get pretty confining when the first fine careless rapture wears off.

So this year we decided not to blow our whole vacation budget on lodge service, when all we need is snow and fresh air. There are many absentee landlords in Vermont who share their vacation homes with other tenants. Our $400 rented us a real Christmas card: a cranberry red farmhouse with a huge kitchen with barnsiding walls and a pot-bellied stove (which we were requested to use only in emergencies, but it was comfortable to look at), a living room with three sides of window view and lots of bedrooms so our children could visit . . . all set in a hundred acres of mountain, meadow and frozen stream.

We could take our dog and cat instead of penning them

in the vet's. We didn't have to get up so "the girl could do the room." We didn't have to dash to the dining room to be on time for breakfast. We didn't have to "wash out our things" in the bathroom sink.

We had somebody else's home complete with all the space and all the machines that our own home has. We had two giant pines and an elm, so placed that the house seems to swing from the trees, as if it could swing clear out to the meadow that sweeps to the mountains. We were so high, we could ski right into the low winter sun where it bewitches the glittering ice-sheathed trees into a forest of chandeliers.

There was a stern sepia photograph of ancestors hanging on the wall, women in tight waists and tight top-knots, men mustached, aloof, a little girl on a sled. It always seems to me that the spirits of people linger in their homes. I could imagine them walking over these wide-boarded floors, stepping out into the snow, a small girl craning out the typical slant Vermont upstairs window.

There was a piano with a bench full of old songs . . . not old, old songs from the times of the people in the picture, but old songs from my own past.

*Over the river and through the trees*
*To Grandmother's house we go.*
*The horse knows the way. . . .*
*Da da da the sleigh*
*Through the white and drifting sno-ow. . . .*

My grandmother lived over the East River. We got there by subway. A long time ago. Grandmothers crowd around the haunted living room. Janet, our youngest daughter, came to spend a few days with us. She stood, reading the unfamiliar scores over my shoulder. Billy and Mick would be up later with the new baby . . . and I would be a grandmother. Tom and Darlene live down the road a piece, across Hungry Mountain.

The beams in this house are made of unplaned trees; they're round as bones. If I had a magical ectoplasm sensitive camera, I could photograph a wierd scene: families and ghosts of families, strangers and beloved, dancing. I began to play, the sun falling bright as snow through the window, beyond a field of alien pine.

*Don't you know that the sun shine . . .*
*All-ways fol-lows the rain. . . . ?*
*So WRAP your troubles in dreams . . .*
*And dream your troubles away. . . .*

I just played the octaves with the right hand. It was one of those encyclopedic music books, each song compacted into its basic melody line. Fake the base. Keep the rhythm faithful. In the simple harmonics of swing, time made tune.

The scene fades. The woman's hands on the keyboard softened to girl's hands. Remove wedding ring. There are many ways of counting time: cancelled checks, birthday parties, husbands ago, wives ago, the year my father had to trade the Lincoln touring car for a Studebaker . . . I count time by songs. When my daughter Janet was very small, we watched a parade together. She looked up and said earnestly, "You know, I feel that music. Here." She pointed to the zipper on her snowsuit.

Music happens. When a musical phrase feeds into a memory bank, old moods return, sharpened by refraction. If I

81

hear Brahms' "Lullabye," Fraulein is singing it, her white starched shoulders, narrow eyes and coiled braid, points of light against the sky: my private constellation. *Guten abend, guten nacht,* syllables strange as sleep, beckon time.

My mother had a crystal powder bowl with a silver lid. On opera nights my father powdered my mother's back and sloped her shoulders into a fleece of ermine and as they swept out the front door, the white fur parted, revealing a peach satin lining, voluptuously private. "Bess," it said, in an embroidered scrawl, the furrier's sign that he had matched these pelts to the exact dimensions of my mother, whose name was Bess.

Our piano also had sloping shoulders, covered in peach satin with an overlay of gold lace (now sleeping in my attic). My mother played all the rapturous soprano arias, and, like Jeanette MacDonald, she also sang operetta. "When I'm calling you-hoo-hoo hoo-hoo-hoo-hoo." Divine tremulo! As Nelson Eddy galloped through the woods in immaculate platinum profile: "I will answer troo-oooo-ooooo." The music of love.

My father had other ideas. Clad in gray pajama top and brown trousers, a dab of shaving cream on his ear and his replaceable tooth perched on the sink like a white and gold spider, he would mush his shaving brush into the lilac mug where his name was written in gold. And then he would snap his fingers and prance and sing: "Rings . . . zon . . . her fingers . . . and bells . . . zon . . . her toes . . ." or "We are tenting tonight on the old campground. . . ." "That's music!" he said.

My *own* music began in the winter of 1936 when our whole high school, four thousand of us, came back from our Christmas vacation. We slogged through the slushy campus where W.P.A. workers slept on their shovels, and we all walked in unison because we were singing: "You blow through here and the music goes down and around—yo-ho-ho-ho . . . ho-ho . . . and it comes out here. . . ."

How foolish that looks on paper. But you've got to hear it. There was scarcely any melody . . . just one or two notes hovering around middle C so that both boys and girls could handle it. But we were just over Christmas; perhaps the music kept the parties going, drowned out blackboard chalk and teacher squawk. "You push that middle valve do—own . . ." (winding through the chill paths we *were* the instrument) . . . "and the music goes down and around. . . . beedle-eee-yo-ho-ho . . . lissen to the jazz come out." It was the *Gone with the Wind* of sheet music. I don't remember any particular professional group singing it. *We* sang it.

And then we danced. The thirties were the years of the Big Bands (who I thought then had always been, would always be). New York was safe and beautiful. We all wore round "bowler" hats like Princess Elizabeth, white gloves, red lipstick, sweaters, pearls. Holiday weekends we "went formal" in long low-cut gowns. Boys had to wear tuxedos at the better hotels.

I can't believe it. With the exception of television, the world has not changed so dramatically in the last forty years. The buildings in the city of New York still shoot for the moon, Central Park is as big and as green, the same traffic clots the street, and the subways still send their hoar breath through manhole covers. But only the shell of the city remains.

Once upon a time . . . in the palm-banked Cinderella Ballroom of the Hotel Roosevelt, Benny Goodman waved the silver wand of his clarinet and we all groaned and held our breath and listened to him play a silver song, "Goodby," a wordless theme song . . . colored spotlights . . . "together dancing," the kids call it today. . . . You rested your head on your date's shirt front—if he were tall enough —and Tommy Dorsey played "polka dots and moonbeams dancing on a pug-nosed dream," the essence of cool daintiness. . . . "I'm getting sent-i-ment-tal . . . over yoooo." Love . . . moon above . . . new moon belonged to June . . . the dip in the dance . . . the cadence. Young men came in rough tweeds with short rough hair and smooth chins. Girls wore stockings and cuban heels and twirling skirts. Only saddle shoes were unisex. . . .

The subways were clean. Times Square smelled of caramel popcorn and jelly apples. Policemen wore spanking white gloves. The only thing you might need a policeman for was to borrow a nickel in case you had no carfare to get home. We walked up town, down town, through the Park, down the broad, deserted, beautiful avenues at any hour, day or night. In the winter they vended hot, hot chestnuts on street corners, in spring gardenias on a velvet board, in summer fresh fruit piled into high, wheeled pushcarts—10 cents.

Among the slow tunes in the ballrooms there were the fast numbers, the jitterbug kids in their saddle shoes and nutcracker legs and twirling hair, solemn-faced, brighteyed. If a couple was particularly good everyone would stop and watch. And then the mass dances came: The Big Apple, The Lambeth Walk from England, the Conga—one-and-two-and three-Kick . . . one-and-two-and-three-KICK! I could never get that straight. I was the only girl in New York too out of step to handle a conga line. I would chat brightly with my date and wonder why he'd asked me out.

But it was fun. Oh, it was fun. . . . September, remember, dying ember . . . "night and day . . . onleee yooo be-neath the moo-oon and under the sun. . . ." The vocabulary was scarcely more complicated than the tunes, but it was so whole-hearted: "You're my yevrething/Underneeth the sun . . . You're my yevrething, rolled dup IN to One." The commitment was absolute: "Everything I have is yours."

New York pulsed neon, sprouted a longitude and latitude of high-rise and highway lights that jitterbugged in a perpetual vaudeville. The city was always ON. A new dish called "pizza," 25¢ a pie, appeared in a chain of Italian restaurants. Hot dogs and giant ice-cold milk-shakes and piña-colada (tropical cocoanut) and cider with waffle sandwiches filled with cream cheese and apple butter . . . gypsy fortune tellers brooding over dark leaves . . . nickels bought everything. Cosmopolitan. Exotic. New York was the spinning hub of a polyglot universe where men blew smoke rings out of billboards and you could never see the stars for the lights of the Great White Way.

My favorite place was the Mayflower Doughnut Shop where in the calyx of tulip glasses they would pour chocolate syrup and then build up: chocolate ice cream, marshmallow sauce, hot fudge (really hot and hardening), whipped cream, a sprinkle of nuts and a cherry . . . and I remember a sign on the wall, painted in what was supposed to resemble illuminated medieval text: "As you wander on through life, brother, whatever be your goal, keep your eye upon the doughnut, and not upon the hole." Not a bad idea.

But nothing lasts. Not the Depression, nor the dreamy swing love tunes. . . . The bright band of lights circling the Times Building spelled out bad news. The War, the faraway war was coming closer. News was no longer funneled cosily and exclusively through Lowell Thomas and Gabriel Heater and H.V. Kaltenborn. During the Saturday night "Hit Parade" and "Saturday Afternoon at the Opera" and Eddie Cantor and Jack Benny and Rudy Vallee you were likely to hear dead silence and then: "We interrupt this program to bring you a special bulletin. . . ." "Munich," "Berchtesgaden," "Anschluss," the "Sudetenland." Broadway had a brownout—lights half-dimmed. The Boardwalk at Atlantic City turned a dark side to the sea. No city here.

And then, during one Sunday afternoon broadcast of the Philharmonic . . . "All members of the armed reserves will report to their units. . . . All members of the armed forces will appear in uniform . . . Pearl Harbor, Pearl Harbor," they said. What a lovely name for a harbor! Irving Berlin wrote "God Bless America" and Kate Smith sang it and so did everybody else. "I Left My Heart at the Stage Door Canteen." "I'll Be Home for Christmas—if only in your dreams. . . ." "When the lights go on again . . . all over the world. . . ."

Bud was drafted. I followed him by Greyhound, and I remember a last look at Times Square. There was a giant —oh, say, thirty foot cardboard cut-out of a young man with his shirt collar boyishly open, his hands turned palm out, and the most winsomely boyish face that had ever been cut out and set against the sequined Broadway sky. And nearby there was a crush of girls in bobby sox and saddle shoes milling under the marquee of the Paramount Theatre. They were waiting for Frankie, to see Frankie *In Person* on the great stage. Fabulous Frankie. Sinatra! whose ingenuous cut-out image dominated the teeming square.

"I've got you . . . under my skin." Sounds like a splinter.

Oh no! Not when Sinatra does it, closing his eyes, holding out those upturned palms, hitting the note just a half tone away from where you'd expect it. That ineffably tender voice could only be meant for a single listener. Frankie never sang to a whole audience; he sang to you, and to you, and, especially, to *you.* He said so. He used to end his radio program that way, and I believed he *was* saying good-night especially to me. And then he'd say, "Good night, Nancy." Such a sweet young husband.

In the autumn of '43, Bud and I went to Miami and Army Air Force Officer Candidate School. Here they had another use for songs: *Sound* off! CAYdence. "Throw a silver dollar down on the ground and it'll roooooolllll—because it's round . . ." "Someone's in the kitchen with Di*nah!* Some-one's in the kitchen I knooooowwwwwowow . . ." "I wanna girl, just like the girl . . . that married dear ol' dad." Left, right, left, right . . . platoon after platoon, right HACE, Harch! Around the corners, faces streaming sweat under the white shoe-polished pith helmets, immaculately fitted suntanned shirts sweat-darkened, all the young men marched singing the old songs from my father's days, my father's war.

I used to lean out the window of my Miami efficiency apartment and wave. But wives were really not welcome and my presence did my husband's candidacy no good. He needed all his time to shine his shoes and his belt buckles, to shave three times a day.

Does a tree crash in the forest if no one hears it? Does a song still play if one person hears it? In that long ago war in those bright hot winter afternoons in the improbable state of Florida, group after group of bright young men turned syncopated corners. Past the posh comandeered ho-

87

tels that were their barracks, past palm trees that were strange to me as the dream of a tree (their bare trunks and fluid branches). *Sound* off. *Sound* off. One two. THREE FOUR. Harch! "Into the yair, Armee Air Force . . . Into the Yair, Piy-lots troooo. . . ." Our war, not my father's.

"Don't sit under the apple tree . . . with anyone else but meeee . . . anyone else but me. . . ."

"I'll be seeing you . . . in all the yold familiar play-ssiss . . ."

". . . no matter what the future brings . . . as time goes by."

And then the war was over. Time to work. No "Pampers." Years of diapers and kids to feed and tell stories to and holler at; books to read, walls to paint, flowers to plant. Romance disappeared along with the foxtrot. I was too busy to fantasize about love. My children grew up and had parties where they danced to rock and roll. Bud and I were fugitives from Elvis Presley and the trembling floor boards of our old house. "The Twist." I could never do the Twist; I could hear no music to move to. Songs became a function of decibel and trick lighting and petulant or inflated lyrics that left me annoyed or unmoved.

Do you have to be "in love" to feel a song?

I played the piano in our rented Vermont house with much pedal, much arpeggio. There were hundreds of songs compressed into the book, typewritten lyrics like a flock of tentative bees over a treble clef fence where notes climbed like roses. I sang about lost love, requited love, forbidden love, love remembered through the black despair of war. Bud and Janet listened. I am strictly a kitchen sink second soprano. But the polished keys took me back . . . back. "Gonna make a sen-ti-men-tal journey. . . .

Se*ven!* Gotta make a train at se*ven* . . . take me back . . . the railroad track. . . ."

In a Vermont garage antique sale I found a pair of green glass candlesticks . . . "$10," the lady said, "These are real depression glass from the thirties." That made me an antique. Later I saw a washboard for $5. Too bad the value of people does not appreciate as they become increasingly antique. Our appetite for the old seems to stop at "things." I guess they're less trouble.

Yet memory welds the past indelibly to the future in odd ways. For instance, we still say "ice-box" and so do our children. Perhaps because my mother never believed in those new-fangled refrigerators even though my father (who was more forward-looking) insisted she buy one. I remember her old wooden ice-box going sadly down to the cellar where it seemed to generate its own cool, and where it could help out at big parties. There was a shelf of cranberry glass tumblers down there also. And today, both that ice-box and those glasses fetch high prices at antique shops. That's something worth thinking about. Why is there that indiscriminate hunger for anything old today—a washboard, a chamber pot, or an old scratched school desk? Do we sense that we've lost something?

There have always been antique collectors. But they hunted fine Chippendale, or Louis XV inlaid tables, hand-rubbed woods, and fine old bronzes. Today if it's old—even paste pearls or moth-eaten furs—it's in demand. I wonder why this is.

But here was the present—already past as I write—forty years—*fifty* years—since Fraulein sang to me. How clear melody hums through the whorls of seashell time. I leafed through the pages of this songbook in a rented vacation house. I sat down at the piano and let my left hand drift over the keys while the right hand picked out the octaves of melody. I sang all the old songs and laughed at the lyrics and my daughter Janet, who is a young woman now and tuned to the new music, came and sang over my shoulder.

"Don't you know that the sunshine . . . all-ways fol-lows the rain? So WRAP (Hold that "WRAP"; fool around with the bass.) your troubles in dreams . . . and dreeeeeeeeeeem your troubles away."

I turned to Janet, self-deprecating, prepared to lay my adolescent sentiment on the altar of our sophisticated camaraderie. But her brown eyes were misted over as she sang.

"That's true," she said. "That's very true."

# PIONEERS: EAST

JUST OVER Hungry Hollow Hill is Tom and Darlene's place, Tom our first-born. I used to count out his cod liver oil drops: one-two-three-four . . . and then I was going to school and asking the teacher to please let him do two-column arithmetic. And now Tom is a computer consultant; he keeps his private computer in the barn. Dials twirl. Cards riffle out with mysterious codes punched on them; sheets swift as old piano rolls crank off their presses. Typewriters compose messages on their own. "Tom," says Detroit, "Chicago is bugging me. He's got his signals crossed. What shall I do?" "Cool it, Detroit," Tom says. And then he tells Chicago to twirl a few dials and press a few circuits.

I know that's not how it goes, but that's what it looks like. It seems to me that just as turtles have their bones exposed for all the world to see, so Tom has his visible thoughts twirling and humming in his office. And I know that because, just like the rest of us, he's got to be in the fresh air, he's tethered his machine to the mountainside. As he communes with his multiple continental connections, water compacted by rock seeps out of the earth, gathers force and comes leaping over Tom's embankment, makes clear green pools, and then broods on towards the sea.

So Tom has many miracles. He is a new breed of pioneer who uses the swiftest forms of transportation and communication to enable him to live on the side of a mountain where he must stake his tomatoes swiftly before frost. The repairman, who came from Boston to fix a few loose circuits looked out the barn door and noticed a deer stealing apples from Tom's tree. "Well, I've seen everything," he said. Perhaps, in a way, he had.

Darlene's kitchen is full of beans and sprouting seeds and flowering geraniums. She's taught Tom to wipe his feet and clean off counters and that's a miracle too. And he's trying to teach her to ski. So far she prefers snowshoes. But it seems to me that the pair of them are possibility incarnate. Do you want something? Simple. Just work for it.

We all decide to go cross-country skiing down the side of Tom's mountain. (Cross-country skiing is all that Bud and I are up to. We're just a couple of over-age ski bums who don't begin to have the nerve or the ability for that rampage known as "downhill.") Tom has a brand-new pair of Christmas skis. We watch him lumbering up the hill like the Abominable Snowman. "See?" he says, "This is how you climb," and he climbs, huge herringbone tracks up the road. "Dig the sides of your skis in." I dig the sides of my skis in, but I slide backwards anyway. I lack the sheer brute strength of my son, the Abominable Snowman.

"Now see this," he says, "Jump turn."

Of course no slender ski could stand that. It broke. But the next day, a kindly ski shop man blamed defective workmanship rather than outrageous skiing, gave him another pair, and up the mountain we went again. Up past the quiet trees, the frozen falls where once we'd found a dead deer, past the terrible gorge where some wanton builder had tried to cut a road, past the strange tracks of snowshoers, on up the quiet fleecy mountain road until Tom gave the signal and we turned and came down—whoosh—fear—into the wind, a ravine to the right where the river runs, down the tender curves, white, sinuous as our summer swans, and more dangerous, until the road leveled slightly and there was Tom's green house and his red Scout and the last stretch is so gentle an incline you have to propel, to glide a little, which I, old lady that I am, prefer although I look back proudly on the ferocities of windy descent once it's over. We ski together on the packed lower roadway snow, till we come to a grey barn, Route 12, and the beginning of another mountain.

Later we ate Darlene's new bread and drove to our rented farmhouse before dark. We kept the spotlight on as I notice everyone does. Otherwise things would be too pitch. It shone on the swing that hangs from the elm tree, and a small company of snowflakes danced around our front door.

We can walk Trinka up here without a leash, and she is very proud of her freedom, does not snap and challenge as she does at home. It's as though she knows she must be responsible for her actions. Sometimes a husky taunts her from his porch. I can see him smirk through his masked eyes. Then I have to remind her firmly that she is a visitor, on her honor. And she trots off to play with a pair of semi-sheepdogs who've come to call. Not so the cat. Jenny hates it. She sits on the stove all day and glares at me. "When are you going home?" she says. "What ever made you think of bringing me to such a dreadful place? No mice, no birds . . . nothing to doooo." I have to throw her out in the morning and when I call her, she's never gone further than beneath the front step.

Sometimes the snow is soft powder, sometimes silver-flecked and wind-rippled as a beach. Trinka is wild with smells, always burrowing, emerging with her narrow muzzle white as a smile. We have learned to ski through virgin field where at first we could only go in snow shoes. The arched prows of my skis throw a fine spray, as if I were walking on water.

But we're not fanatic cross-country skiers. There's no need to fall. We go at our own pace, on our own trail. We're not like those Norwegian eager beavers, whizzing by in scarlet knickers, poles flailing. We don't need "a light, a flask, and an extra tip" or even a companion, as the safety regulations insist for the formal marked trails.

We never skied for more than an hour or so, never so far that we couldn't walk home easily if a ski broke. And we never had any of the slippery packing of a much-used trail. We barely attempt to punt like a gondolier—push off alternate ski and pole—none of that invigorating routine. Bud's doctor has warned him that skiing might be overdoing it. *Time* magazine this January printed a cozy little "milestone" about a chap who dropped dead of a heart attack while cross-country skiing. So we are wary. When we tire, we just shuffle along, dragging our poles or tucking them under our arms like briefcases. We're much more like a pair of boulevardiers than the traditional Alpine forge aheaders.

But it is impossible for me to believe there is anything but health in these clear white winter days. Our tired indoor spirits really get nourishment from the sturdy pines and apple trees that flank our path. It is as though they were meant to say—"look, endure, we're here forever, and life is longer than you think." I knew a doctor who planned his hospitals so that patients were wheeled into surgery—not half comotose in an elevator as bare as a grave—but taken through a garden to a separate wing of the hospital, so that their impressions before pain would be those of beauty. The earth may have been given to man to "tend and subdue." But the good gardener knows his plants. He speaks to them and attends their answer. "Hush," says the snow on the meadow. "Watch," says the sharp dip between fields. "Wait," say the buds clenched like tiny fists on the dogwood, "we're scheduled to be among the first and we're ready, but we can't jump the gun or we'll die."

After our fashion, we managed swifter downhill slopes and easy turns. I, as usual, had terror to cope with. And terror tenses and makes awkwardness; you lose your balance and fall. I hate to fall. I would rather not try something than fail—which is stupid. I hate to be afraid. I would stand on the brow of a hill and look at the beautiful dizzy descent —not more than thirty feet, say 30 degrees, nothing to a real skier. But to me, it represented both a challenge and the ultimate abyss. Bud is braver. He'd go down a long driveway that bordered our field, and I went down it too. But ski conditions change. Sometimes the crust of snow melts and then freezes, and although the surface looks the same, you are skiing on ice and not snow. But Bud, once he conquers his original reluctance, will not be stopped. Then he has to prove he's the boy he once was, the one who walked on girders, and always took a dare. So down the glass hill he went, faster and faster and faster until his descent was broken on a mound the snowplow had deposited.

And then I saw him, heavy jacket flapping open because

he was warm, walking up the hill holding his skis in his hand. He had snapped off the point of his ski. It was so funny, so sad, such a mixture of exultance and rue . . . he and Tom are so much alike. Who ever heard of a gene for breaking skis? I did. Let the behaviorists attribute everything to environment; any parent knows better.

I learned to go downhill finally, taking the hill less and less tangentially. And I learned to know the exultation of pure speed, when you are literally weightless, lying on the wind. We prowled through forests that teetered on the mountain ridge. We brushed against the pine needles and smelled the sweet green. Trinka made trails for us to follow, or broke our trails on the open fields, or tried to hitch a ride on the back of our skis. We felt as capable as swallows and curious as wolves . . . and best of all, in touch, freed from the prison of our familiar selves. We didn't have to feel responsible for the snowfall and the tree growth. Someone, with infinite generosity, had given us a gift of these days.

As we progressed, we discovered something not mentioned in any cross-country ski manual. We discovered stopping.

To do this, you stand perfectly still. The landscape roots. You see snow just blossomed on apple trees, tall pines dragging their blankets Indian file down hill. There are the mountains, Glen Ellen and Sugarbush; I love strange names. Who was Ellen? An old wise grandmother or a young mad girl who lived in a glen on the mountain? A sugarbush, a cookie, a metaphor for a bush covered with snow? No. I look that one up. A "sugarbush" is a grove of maples used for brown sugar and maple syrup. And that's nice. I've seen the heavy wooden buckets that tap the trees like quiet woodpeckers, the hauling sleds and the great barrels that hold the rendered sap. I like to think of a quiet working mountain. The dictionary gives as alternate word, "sugar orchard." It certainly looks all spun of sugar now. Glen Ellen and Sugarbush are tall mountains—now you see them; now you don't. A white river of ski trail, like a gash, is suddenly visible where a minute ago there was only pearl cloud. Sometimes clouds pretend to be mountains, just as blue and humped. And sometimes the blue humped mountains get hazy as clouds. And sometimes you look across the meadow and see nothing at all. The meadow could be a jumping off place for the edge of the world.

And—as suddenly (They say in Vermont: "If you don't like the weather, wait a minute.")—a shaft of sunlight scours the horizon, dusts off the mountains and brings them back. But the view will still be blocked by smoke from signal fires in the valleys where moisture, gray as smoke, condenses and returns dreamily to the clouds from whence it came. And this is another of these circular miracles: how the sound of fire and the sound of waves and the sound of wind through leaves is so similar when such different elements are involved—how mist which is so wet should look like smoke which is so dry; how dry ice is so cold it burns.

It seems to me that God says, "Come back. You may go just so far with your 'true selves,' your individual identity and caprice." But basically the world is one. There is One Spirit that infuses all. The further you seem to diverge, the closer you come. Hot is cold and dry is wet and wind moves all things, turns rock to earth to flower to earth to rock, turns death to life and life to death. So the world rocks in the great circle of paradox. A pendulum is limited by the spring from which it hangs; witless, it may go just so far, then return."

Here at the top of the world all city reality blows away in a lace tracery of maple. The clear print of a cloven hoof attests to a deer, and I can understand the myth of Diana, bathing, guarded from the sight of mortals by her nymphs. Because, as the story goes, Acteon, a hunter, witnessed her secret rites. Diana, who was in charge of both the hunt and chastity, promptly changed this peeping Tom into a stag, who was then torn by his own hounds. And here is the print of deer among our own dog's tracks. And, as we stand still, I can even hear the splashing water—yes I can!

Thaw comes in sporadic rushes, then thinks better of it and retreats. I thought spring was a sudden irreversible rush. It is not. Spring comes tentatively tapping, afraid to get her feet wet, her hands chilled. You hear the crack of frost way before you see it when spring is far away, just as there is a long pause between the sight and sound of lightning in a distant storm: secret affinities, parallel receding lines seem to converge. In the curve of the world they actually do. Seeing is believing.

So, in January the year has tilted. Sun and earth know. The weather hesitates. The rush towards chill that was December confuses the January tip to spring. There've been days of silent freeze and others where ravines reveal themselves in turbulent washaway snow. I've seen sea green pools with three inch-rims of ice, or an alligator-shaped skin of stubborn freeze, finally freed, swimming dissolvingly away. I've heard the sullen thud of floes that dropped over Tom's waterfall. God is logging, sending down timbers to build up the sea.

"No. It sounds like Titans," Tom says. "Titans below the earth. Hear them drink." It does sound like that. Great glugs. But Tom is more pioneer than mythologist. He bought that waterfall for the same reason he bought the computer: to attain a measure of independence. He doesn't want to be at the mercy of price-gouging energy brokers. He wants to make a self-contained unit on the side of his mountain. He's drawing up plans for a generator. He wants to harness the river and kindle his own lamps.

Last fall, we were walking his property, we two. It's the kind of land into which so many rivers have cut so many gorges that walking is a continual battle with slippery leaves —going up or going down. Tom and I like that sort of thing. It makes me feel young, and I love to watch him because he is both nimble and clumsy as a bear, bear-shaped, bear-bearded and bear-determined.

So finally, as we walked, the land on the other side of the stream became irresistible. But how to cross? There was a natural ford, about six inches deep, eight feet wide, with enough stepping stones for a giant. "Can you leap, mother?"

"Absolutely not."

"Then I'll build you a bridge."

I set out to watch my modern Sir Walter Raleigh spread a bridge, instead of a cape. And of course I felt like a queen.

First he took huge boulders and threw them in the water. And I took a picture of him throwing huge boulders into the water. All very prehistoric, his beard, his bark-colored shirt, the great splash of the indignant boulders. "Put one there," I would say. And he would. "Now, one more— there." And he would. But no bridge of stepping stones appeared.

Here we were, both considered to be highly intelligent

problem solvers, by our own estimation. We couldn't make the kind of bridge that was child's play to beavers. "Beavers!" Tom said, reading my thoughts.

"Beavers," I agreed. And we set to work hauling a few drowned trees along the shore to our ford, and he threw the drowned trees in and redrowned them. And still no bridge appeared.

"Mother," he said. "Look." I looked. "We're filling in a pool and raising the water level."

It was marvellous to be so wrong. I still don't know exactly why the water didn't run obediently around our jetty. But it didn't. I love to see the red light flash on man's great schemes. Even Tom's. We walked merrily through the water. It was cool, actually, a pleasant path. And I shall always remember that a few of the stones in the riverbed Tom rents from the Lord are a watery cairn commemorating a jolly afternoon.

One day I went into Montpelier to shop, and I had the feeling I should have changed travelers' checks for foreign currency (as we often do on vacations), and then I realized with pleasure that everyone spoke English.

We got a temporary library card, noticed three lovely Wyeth watercolors hung, with typical New England understatement, in the library foyer. Like tourists we visited the Historical Museum and were struck, as usual, by the rich but brief history of our country.

There were geological displays, a few Indian artifacts. Vermont entered the United States right after the Revolution—after Canada and New Hampshire and New York had relinquished their claims to it. Then state history becomes cosy.

There were the axes of Ethan Allen and his Green Mountain "Boys," enormous axes that only giants could have carried and yet we know the men were shorter then. The first cross-country skis leaned against the wall, twenty-five feet long; one would be more catamaran than skier on those. There was a small replica of a doctor's office with his appointment book open and a spidery handwriting: "Mrs. Eliza Jones . . . attended. . . . $10. Rufus King, powders, 25¢." Not many patients in any one day, and then you realized each patient had to be reached by horse and buggy; there probably wasn't much hurrying you could do. We passed under the stern faces of ladies in frivolously ruffled caps staring from ancestral portraits. There was a sign, "Please Touch," on a display of early tools: a ruffling iron, a tooth puller, a sausage stuffer.

We saw none of the ancient artifacts, the jewels or the weaponry of a European museum. This seemed a testament to a peaceful people trying to live decently in a climate where none but the fit could survive. The museum recorded only a few generations from home. As a matter of fact, some of the tea cups and shaving mugs had little index cards beside them: "When I was a girl Mrs. Casey used to serve my mother out of these cups."

Fresh from our city fears and suburban wariness, we were struck by the easy-going courtesy of the Vermonters in the stores, in the streets, waving as they skidded by on the snowy roads. Sometimes they would stop and kindly offer assistance; pedestrians are rare on their winter roads. But there are nights in Vermont when the moon is so bright on the white-washed snow, and the stars twinkle with the diamond pointillism of sun splintered on water, and because of the strange reversal of bright earth and darker sky, you feel as though you are walking on the bright crust of the moon, walking in some time not known to man. You drink great splashes of blue night and the frost of your breath dances like a private snow flurry when you speak.

But there's a snake in every garden. Perhaps that's an integral part of the nature of gardens. I don't know, but Bud and I had a problem. Our problem was that we had no real problems anymore. Our period of life-and-death concern with the children is over. The mortgage is paid. That wolf who used to howl at our doorstep has slunk away. Having fewer people and fewer concerns in our day, we have more time to watch each other.

And this is particularly true on vacation when our normal routines have switched. Not that we get in each other's hair. I've heard women say, "For better or for worse, but not for lunch." As a free lance writer, Bud has usually been home for lunch, and that has always been a pleasant interval.

What has happened is that I used to do all the "woman's work," because Bud was the breadwinner, and I willingly accepted the house as my responsibility. But when the children no longer came home for lunch, I felt there wasn't enough to keep me home full-time. I went back to college, got the necessary degrees to become a professor of English, and for the past nine years I've been teaching. Not a nine-to-five away job, but plenty of papers to mark at home.

Here comes the feminist argument: why shouldn't the man help? If the woman is bringing in the money as well as the man, shouldn't the man take care of the dirty dishes as well as the woman? He feels that his prerogatives are threatened; she feels that hers are abused. It can turn nasty, particularly without the poultice of daughters around. Pam and Janet have been fine arbiters for us.

Now we were alone, quite alone, no buffer zone, no one between us and the small but insistent household chores that need doing. After dinner, for instance, I would say: "Aren't you going to clean off the counter?"

"Aren't you?"

"Aren't *you* going to do *anything?*" In all justice, Bud does most of the cooking but I think that is the pleasanter part of the job. Who wouldn't rather cook than clean?

Bud: "Why do you always have to shatter a pleasant hour with your niggling, irritating demands?"

Me: "Why do you always find my demands irritating?"

Bud: "Why do you have such a knack for spoiling things?"

Me: "Why don't you help more?"

Bud: "I do."

Me. "You don't." I follow this up with an itemized list of his latest faults and some from ten or twenty years back that happen to come to mind.

His face gets blacker and blacker, black eyes snapping sparks till I think his beard will ignite. He picks up the garbage and stalks out, Trinka loyally at his heels. He comes back in again, tracking snow.

"Take off your boots," I say.

"It's no use, Dorothy," he says. (When he calls me "Dorothy," I know it's serious; usually it's just "Dorth," a name only he uses. I love it.) "It's just not working out. I think you'd rather go off and live by yourself and not bother with housekeeping anymore. You've changed. Obviously you've got lots of festering resentments. Maybe you're right. I'm not the world's best husband. But I can't go on this way."

I look at him. He still has his snowy boots on. He's leaning against the door with the garbage can in his hand. His parka juts out from his Old King Cole girth and his beard is meshed with the gray of his fur-lined hood. He has such a warm toy shape. He barks like a bear, but he has the soul of a Giant Panda. And he looks so sad.

Suddenly I explode with laughter: "Not working out! After thirty-three years he decides we're not working out! Why we're the best-matched couple we know and you know it!" I collapse laughing against the sink. "Not working out indeed! If we can't make it, I don't know who can!"

The tension drains out of his face and the smile returns. It is a wistful, winsome smile—the same smile he wore a thousand years ago when he asked me out on our first date (which I had to maneuver him into asking). "You'll go with me?" he said then. I can still hear it. "You'll go with me?" He was so eager. "Of course," I said coolly.

And that was the end of that argument. But what he was saying was that I am not as acquiescent or as solicitous as I used to be. And that is true. So he thinks that because he is catered to less, he is loved less. And that is false. But how to solve it?

Rage is easy, but no solution. Separation would be ridiculous. Our commitment to one another and to the children is much too great. And besides we are each the one person the other would most like to be marooned on a desert island with.

What to do?

There are kinds of consciousness that cannot be raised by

discussion. I watched Tom and Darlene as they came to visit us in our toy house, or when we went to visit them. The boy that I sent into the world—let's face it—was not house-broken. I absolutely lost the battle to keep his room neat at home. His housemaster at Andover, a very orderly Navy man, would gladly have shut Tom in a brig, but Andover had no brig. A visit to Tom's apartment when he was out in the world always involved housekeeping for the girls and/or me. And yet here was this slip of a girl with the soft, soft voice, and here was this same Tom—*doing* the dishes, wiping up spills! Actually, mother-in-law wise, I don't see why a man with an outside-the-house job has to help a woman with an inside-the-house job. But objectively, Tom is big and strong, and works at a desk all day. A little congenial exercise can't do him any harm.

The big question for me was: how does she do it? And, why can't I do the same thing? I listened. I watched them. And then I think I found the magic signal. Every time she asks him to do something she either prefaces it or adds an affectionate syllable: "Dear, will you put out the garbage?" "Will you bring in the butter, sweetheart?" "Scrub this pot, love." She cinched it for me when they came to dinner. I was cleaning up and Darlene was helping, and she said, "Tom, did you come here to watch your mother work?" Her voice was very soft.

Actually, they came for dinner. I enjoy cooking for them, and I don't mind cleaning up. But I must say it was more pleasant to clean up together, and less work for me, and not more than a token for Tom.

So, says I to Bud, why don't we try saying this "dear" and "sweetheart," and let's see what happens?

"Why don't you just do it and not tell me you're doing

it, so I'll think you're sincere?" he grumbled.

"Because I'm not the only one that's supposed to say it. You have to call me 'sweetheart,' too."

Sounds ridiculous after being married for thirty-three years. But everything else about life changes, so why shouldn't attitudes?

And what really amazes me is that it does work. Bud has a very low boiling point, ignites to rage in a second. But I suddenly realized that most of the cause of his rage was a sense of being belittled—if I made an offhand suggestion, or requested some lowly chore. And—the corollary I had never connected, he is equally vulnerable on the other end if the spectrum: say one nice word to him, and he is yours.

So slowly, the snapping routine of our days abated. "Dear, will you . . . ?" The self-consciousness dropped from our voices. We began to really believe what we were saying. Why shouldn't we address each other fondly? Why should intimacy destroy courtesy? Men and women are bound to have problems. If he had suddenly decided to change his lifestyle as I decided to change mine, if, for instance, he took a job that pulled him out of the house much more than I am accustomed to, I would have to make some adjustment. I think too many women today act as though they must make a change to solve some old grievance, and then that the poor husband must follow helter skelter however he can.

But men don't shift gears that easily. I remember the *Ladies' Home Journal* used to say (when it dared), "Marriage is a Woman's Business." I still think we know more about it. Even the statisticians have to admit that women, as a rule "test" better at personal and verbal communications, that men do better with abstractions and numbers. And I know,

I feel "in myself" better when I can handle a problem like a "lady" and not like a termagant. It's really nice to call someone "dear." It's a pleasant word to respond to. After a while you discover you really mean it.

And then it was time for company. Vacation homes become more "home" as more family arrives. We had Janet, Tom and Darlene, and now the robin's-egg-blue Datsun with the "Tourista" Mexican sticker still on the windshield arrived from Maine, Mick and Bill looking rather immigrant-like, hooded, much luggage, and Mick with a bundle of blankets in her arm. I went to the door.

She handed me the bundle. "Here's a present for you."

There she was. Tanya. Just as they had described her— apricot skin, dark trusting eyes, even then that exquisite modeling, that sense of mystery that marks a little girl baby. "Oh, Micki, isn't she beeyootiful? Oh, isn't she?" What are the words? There are none. Sometimes you feel your heart's on target. That's all. Bill, hulking sheepishly in the background, Mick's dark eyes, bright as Tanya's, the bright smell of their cold coats and the little fledgling bundle in my arms.

I carried her upstairs, a good excuse for a long hug, and went to the room where Bud was working. "Bud," I said, "someone's come to see us."

We all went for a walk on the virgin roads that are not plowed because no one lives on them. Tanya slept in a pack on Bill's chest like a kangaroo baby. Sometimes she'd cock one dark eye and look at the world and then she'd think better of it and go back to sleep.

We walked in woods that are quiet as paintings, every

tree in place. Bill and Janet shinnied up the slender birch trees till the trees bent under their weight and they swung out into space, feet free, hanging by their hands like monkey-people, and leaped to the ground.

I'd never seen anyone do that. All these years I'd been reading and teaching Robert Frost's poems, "Birches" and "Stopping by Woods on a Snowy Evening." I'd been trying to explain to my city-based students what it must be like to swing free from a tree that is so supple it bends with you, that will break if you climb too high, will not bend if you don't climb high enough, so that you have to be brave, but not foolhardy. And you have to choose your tree wisely, find one that is not too old and fat and stiff, nor too young and thin and weak. So we were looking for the loveliest young birches.

Oh, it was like walking with Robert Frost: "to see his woods fill up with snow," understanding what he meant when he said, "one could do worse than be a swinger of birches." Trees and clouds and my climbing children scribbled visible poems on the white pages of the new snow. Every tree had a circular clearing at its base where the warm breath of the tree had actually melted the snow. I never knew a tree breathed.

"Here," said Bud, "man has been." A creeper-festooned derrick hid in the bushes chomping on a load of snow. We walked by a farm where they kept horses and in the fresh snow their backs were limned white in the same rolling contours as the mountains, as though they were all drawn by the same Artist. He seems to like curves.

Watchdog geese barked and bullied. I saw a miser tree that still held its apples, red as Christmas balls. Down in the orchard, I knew, buds were swelling, visible winter dreams of summer crops. Is a bud the dream of a tree? Are dreams true? Sometimes? When the circuits are wired correctly? Someone once said, "A prophet has a memory for the future." That's a wild one. If time is a curve, can you rise above it and see tomorrow? Perhaps, when you stand on the crest of a wave of love.

We walked back to the house and said softly to one another, what we have said so many times, "It's criminal for us to fight amid such wealth."

# WORKING WOMEN

AT Westchester Community College, spring term begins in February. For me this is exactly the right time to begin a term because I have this thing about light, that seems to enter all my activities. I love the way we greet each of the darkening months with a holiday, a holiday that becomes more meaningful as the days darken. That means that as an autumn housewife I can busy myself planning parties, anticipating the arrival of children, baking, doing the inside things I can not bear to do in spring.

When Halloween comes, there is no question that the year is approaching the end. This is further certified by Thanksgiving. And the deepest darkness heralds the Light of Christmas—which is one of those Divine happy paradoxes that holds the world on keel for me.

But anyway, after January, I have had enough of celebration and am eager to get back to work. And then I began to think about that. I love my home. I am never bored. I began to work only when there were no more children to take care of at home. It was pleasant to be able to add a regular base to Bud's feast-or-famine free-lance income. But I resented outside authority, having to please strangers, having regular hours—especially in the morning, because I function best from noon to midnight.

I am terrified of driving in bad weather, and there is no other way I can get to my school. Once the term begins, I really work around the clock, reading papers that are not always fascinating, doing all the humdrum minutia that is essential for anyone who works as part of an institution. I feel very strongly that the woman with children at home who need her, should not look longingly at her sister out there in the "world." The world out there is not that great. It can wait.

But working has some advantages. It gives a woman a chance to slip out of one personality into another, to actually doff an old role and assume a new one. The very essence of mothers is that they are always there, familiar and dependable. Since mothers have very few arbitrary deadlines, they can usually stop what they're doing to help: to deliver or pick up a person or a parcel, whip up a dress or a dessert, perform some emergency household repair, answer the telephone and stay fastened to that cord for too long, or simply be interrupted by dog, cat, child, or neighbor. All this has its compensations. The day I feel that no one needs me, that no one calls on me for anything, will be (I hope) the day I retire from this stage. It's nice to be part of a bustling community. The saddest people in the world are those who are so free that no one knows—or cares—whether they're around or not.

But it's also nice to be someone else sometimes, to respond, yes, but to a different set of demands. I would hate to live in a world where I was only addressed by my formal name, my "anyone's" name, the one that appears on forms.

I would hate to give up the special endearments only husbands are allowed, or that bleated "Maaaaa!" that the children still use as they open the front door and call up the steps. I would hate to live in a world surrounded only by the sheathed assessing eyes of strangers.

But there is also a psychic relief to anonymity. I think the woman's movement puts too much stress on the "real Me." There really can be no uninvolved self. But I think it is a relief to have some involvements that are superficial, that do not require the emotional pull that love always exerts. I used to use crafts for this when I was home full time. I still sew and garden and clean cupboards partly to relax. The white hot glare of concentrating on beloved people, even when this brings pleasure, can, unrelieved, be a drain.

It is nice to live life on many levels. If I had to make a choice, I would choose family, of course. But there is no necessity for choice. Life is long enough for both. So come February I put away my "playclothes," wax skis and boots and memories, dress in jewelry and heels "like a lady" and drive up the winding Hutchinson River Parkway to work —hoping that it will snow only on weekends.

I like the drive—because it is beautiful, because my car knows the way by now, and because I have a chance to brood—over lessons, events, things I have read or will write. Take the article in *McCall's* June, 1975. It was entitled "Why Woman's Work is Never Done." It's only two columns long, so it could scarcely be as definitive as the title suggests. Anyway, here are some amazing statistics. Nonworking women spend fifty-five hours a week on housework, as contrasted with the employed woman who spends twenty-six hours. *McCall's* is forgetting that the employed woman spends at least another fifty hours working and travelling to work, bringing her grand total up to seventy-five!

The article goes on to say that the average woman spends six hours a week doing her laundry nowadays when she only spent five hours a week fifty years ago! I know that twenty years ago I spent at least three hours a week just ironing—something that is quite gone since perma-press. Thirty years ago I washed by hand every day and fifty years ago in my mother's house washing took all Monday, ironing hours of Tuesday. Who spends even six hours a week on laundry? Don't you ever wonder who tabulates statistics? Sometimes I think sociologists collect data the way a miser collects money—without too careful scrutiny of sources.

To continue, *McCall's* explains that the non-working woman's "house-working" hours include eight hours a week of "family care," talking to children, etc. I do not see how the care of human beings can be measured along with the care and waxing of the kitchen floor. A child is a *person,* just as my pupils and my colleagues are persons—but with one significant difference. A child is a person to whom the parent has a lifetime commitment. The child who is reared by a nursemaid or a succession of day care teachers will never have the emotional security of the child who knows his or her mother cared enough to stay home. And the mother is depriving herself of the pleasure of really knowing and aiding in the growth of her own child.

Any psychologist will say that the first five years are the most important. Indeed the first year, the first months are of consummate importance because this is the time that basic response patterns are set. An infant's brain is almost clear. All the connections are to be made. You can literally see how the response to light, to sound, to a face, to love grows with each day.

The *McCall's* article concluded with the question of self justification. It says the reason that "unemployed" (can you accept the designation "unemployed" for a full-time home-maker?) women work longer hours is to demonstrate, perhaps unconsciously, "the importance of their work so that their husbands will value them more. Working women do not feel this pressure."

I couldn't believe the article ended with such an outrageous unqualified statement, but it did. Aren't most employee's activities directed towards conspicuous importance? Imagine the employee or the boss who will say, "Never mind what I did today. It was all a waste of time." The employee would be fired; the boss would go bankrupt. And what is wrong with wanting to be valued by your employer or your husband? Husbands also want to be valued by their wives. At the heart of every good relationship, I think you will find each party trying to be of some value to the other.

It is only the spoiled child who follows his own instincts without regard to anyone else's feelings. And sometimes I think even the tantrum of the spoiled child is a cry for control, a request for the parent to step in and demand some acceptable behavior. When we love someone, it is natural to want to be of value to them. It is also a way of saying "thank you," for the beloved person is of value to us.

Once I spoke to young people in a psychology class in Manhattan Community College. I remember the invitation. It said: "I understand you have written a book *against* the woman's liberation movement. If this is not a misprint, would you care to come and address my class?" I was grateful for the invitation, but deeply sorry for the girls. "Children are no more than dirty diapers," they said. "Housework is just an endless mound of dirty dishes."

One girl in the front row raised her hand and said very softly, so no one would hear, "I'm with you. I want to stay home and raise my own children." How would these young people know what they are giving up so blithely, so fiercely? Obviously they have never been mothers, and what they have seen at home has not been what psychologists would call "positive role reenforcement." "My mother felt trapped." "She didn't want me." "She's never home."

The girls in this class—and many classes like it—are the victims of the angry voices of women (teachers, writers) who can't take (or don't have) the pressures of home—the self-motivation and the self-discipline—who need certification by paycheck to give meaningful structure to their hours.

I have often wondered if I would keep my house clean if no one ever set foot in it. It would certainly not be with the same pleasure. I like my house to be pleasing to the people who come in to it—not because it gives me a sense of importance, but because my house is an extension of my own personality, like my clothes, or my speech. I would not walk around in a dirty dress. I do not like to be caught in a dirty house. Not because it makes me feel unimportant, but because it makes me feel unattractive. This does not mean that I always achieve the standards that I set. But I try.

It's agreeable to please. Smiles are contagious. I think we need more of this so-called feminine self-effacing, and less "masculine" aggression. There is too much "Me me me!" We need more "we." As soon as you say "we," pleasing comes naturally. And that's another place where family training is crucial. A family is the basic community, the first step to meaningful participation in the community outside. This is woman's work—if she is home to do it. A child cannot learn "we" from a succession of day-care teachers who are working, after all, for money and not for love.

"Some women just don't like children." I've heard that one often. "If you're the kind of person who prefers adults, it is better to turn your child over to a young-person-oriented teacher until the child is old enough for you to relate to yourself." I have actually heard this, not from a monster, but from a sincere woman, repeating what she'd heard.

I think some women do not naturally coo effusively over tiny babies. This should not be confused with lack of love. Different teachers, I know, prefer different grades. Certainly people have varying affinities. But this is quite different from denying your own flesh and blood!

I think babies have had a bad press these days. At parties people used to ask, "How many children do you have?" If the answer was "None," your interlocutor would cluck sympathetically. Now the question is, "What do you *do?*" meaning, of course, at what are you gainfully employed. If you answer, "I don't do anything," or you try to explain that you are a full-time self-employed home economist, you will not even get the sympathy the childless woman was once accorded. You'll get downright scorn. "What? Do nothing all day? How do you *stand* it? I'd climb the walls."

Young women are sensitive creatures. Who isn't? Hear something often enough and it becomes convincing. So young mothers will observe that their babies do certainly and repetitively stain their diapers, spill their milk, "get into things," ask questions, disobey, whine and require watching. The natural rewards of a smile, a hug, an accomplishment—peek-a-boo, a tower of blocks, a song learned—evaporate before the diminution of status in the eyes of the world. "You're just a mother! How can you stand it?" Oh, woe, how can I stand it indeed? I want to be a ballerina! I want to be doctor!

According to the new McGraw-Hill guidelines for aspirations, a little girl should also be able to say, "I want to be a fireman, astronaut, plumber . . ." as though any of these activities were without constricting routines—or as varied or important as mothering. The woman at home knows, although she doesn't think of it in her frustrated rage, that no job can be done without discipline. But she resents the discipline of her own home, because home has lost its status.

That's where the women's movement has done a disservice, has been anti-feminine. We need mothers. We need good mothers more than any other single category of occupation. We need fathers too, but I think, at least in the early years, there must be a sexual division of responsibility. After all, fathers do not become pregnant; they do not nurse children; they do not secrete maternal hormones. There seems to be a higher law than even the Equal Rights Amendment can legislate which says that where young children are concerned, women are *not* equal. They need their old-fashioned protected preferential status: they need financial support.

But a young woman also needs to feel that the job she is doing with her child is important. I know a young physical therapist who works with severely brain-damaged children. She spends all day moving her small patients' hands from left to right. If she is successful, some of them may, some day, learn to initiate the movement on their own. But she does not feel her job is boring or useless. This young physical therapist has her status certified by paycheck and by society, and I have heard her say to a young mother, "How can you bear to be cooped up with that baby all day?" What can that young mother answer? She doesn't know what it's like "out there." She only hears inflated reports: "Working people have such interesting days," she says. "I can only say, 'I took the children to the playground.'"

But home can be a tool of thought, a philosophy, to use elegant "educational" terms. Homemakers turn thought into process and memory. How many times have I heard a student say, "I can't remember. I read a page in a book and then I forget it. What did I do last week? I forget. Don't ask." I think we forget what we have no reason to remember; we forget facts that have no real meaning to us. And, the more passively we live our lives, the more we watch, the less we do, the more we fill our days with trivia about people and ideas we do not love—the less need we have to remember. And then where has yesterday gone? And all the busy empty years? For the home-centered, process reenforces memory. Activity has catalogued the years. Responsibility has ruled out passivity. And we perceive with our trained senses and our past experience.

Even college, these days, is giving credit for "life experience." Home is certainly the living laboratory, the workshop, the stage, the on-the-job training program and the garden where children flower. It's nice out in the world— if you have an interesting job—I'd like to tell young mothers. You'll get there, if you want to. But meanwhile someone's got to mind the store. In your store, at home that is, there are some mighty important customers—your children. And they are learning language, logic, response, responsibility, love and art. And you're the professor, the president and the custodian of America's first line university: the home.

That's what I'd like to tell young mothers. Careers are always there. Children grow up and disappear. Have both —there's plenty of time for each, one at a time.

I like my school. I like the serious young men and women. I like the fact that it is a *community* college, *my* community, so that I am part owner and part employee and sometimes my neighbors are my students. And I like the fact that, because Westchester is a community college, we try to reach the whole community and not only the standard college-age population. That means we encourage educational innovations and, since I endorse this, I teach special classes—sometimes in the penitentiary to prisoners, sometimes in the precinct house to policemen, sometimes in school to the "standard mix."

This particular February I elected to meet a Saturday non-credit course in "Effective Communication," not quite sure what that means, but always glad to give a new idea a whirl.

Thirteen women showed up, and two men. They seemed to be early middle-aged, middle income, some professional, one retired, some thinking of becoming professional. They'd had no homework, no text, since this was the first class. And I had three hours to fill. They'd paid me to fill their morning.

I began by writing my name on the board four ways: Professor, Mrs., Ms., and Miss. I planned to start a discussion about the meanings of words by asking them which title they'd be most comfortable with. "Professor," they said, opting for the formal structure. We had a bit of discussion about "Ms." or "Mrs." but it never really perked. Then a new student arrived. I asked her name. "Harriet Winters."

"Well," I said, "Harriet, which of these names would you like to call me?"

She was a slender dark woman, about my height (5'5"), with the kind of long definite face I think I have. "The name that's not on the board," she said, without a moment's hesitation.

I was at a loss.

"You called me 'Harriet.' I'd like to call you by your first name."

Then the class really woke up. I wrote "Dorothy Evslin" on the board. For me, it was as though the classroom had become a revolving stage and I became a new character, no longer the isolated conductor. It is the non-credit, I think. They are sure enough of themselves to proceed without formal evaluation, and I am delighted to be relieved of the arbitrary responsibility of turning judgments into numerical equivalents.

We had a good session—three hours with no break. They even voted to go without a break next time! We worked with nouns and verbs: finding the precise modifier-eliminators. "Say 'amble' if you mean 'walk slowly.' Never say 'shoe.' If a shoe is worth mentioning at all, let it be a boot, a thong, a platform." They noted that. It is amusing to me to see which of my great truths they consider noteworthy. In the catalogue it said this course would "improve skills in listening and note taking."

As an assignment, I charged them to write down "what you see on the way home." And they responded, just as my younger students had, "Don't do too much looking on the way home. You'll have an accident."

The following week, dutifully, they brought me: "puddles of gravel where the mud gains over the water and a beer can gives a metallic answer" . . . "a white cloud of snow broken by trees". . . . One man and woman had lunched together and gave very different accounts of what was obviously an enjoyable meal. . . . One woman wrote of her terror of the icy road . . . another of her great fear of being late and worrying her husband. (Some ladies pounced on this. Apparently the writer had violated one of the new taboos. She was still insisting, like a pre-Friedan female, that her presence be indispensable to her husband.) But she had constructed a beautiful paragraph about her arrival at home and it was obvious that she and her husband are still in love—always nice to hear. . . .

Then there was a student who was so preoccupied with her assignment that she went to a parking lot, spent ten minutes trying to start a car and suddenly discovered the car wasn't hers, wasn't even a blue one like hers. But when she finally arrived home, she wrote that "her dog and a flock of blackbirds had tracked a message in Morse code on her snowy lawn."

"What a lovely metaphor!" I said. "A real poem."

I watched her write a pleased little note to herself.

I was glad they called me by my first name. After all, we are peers, these middle people and I. It makes school that much more like home.

# THE BIBLE IN THE BACKYARD

EVERY YEAR, punctually after Christmas and the winter solstice, the seed catalogues arrive, promising a Spring more fragrant, a summer more breath-taking, and a harvest more abundant than ever. Like squirrels savoring their winter hoard, we gardeners pore over the pages of Burpee, Stern, Scott, Park, et al. Winds howl. Branches crack under ice. Cold seeps through the thermopane. And the distant sun takes a short cut over our grim winter sky.

But it doesn't matter. We are reading: "Thrill to the incomparable beauty of clouds of blossoms smothering every branch and branchlet. . . . Vigorous, will thrive where other plants fail. . . . Blooms measuring six to eight inches in diameter. . . . You will be the envy of your friends . . . Just a few minutes to plant for a lifetime of beauty. . . . Disease and drought resistant."

Who can resist such appeals?

Catalogue strawberries, tomatoes, peas and beans promise to twine themselves verdantly still, producing bushels of photogenic fruit. Zucchini and asparagus grow on platters, sometimes accompanied by a flowering hollandaise. Whose palate is so jaded it does not lust for "paw-paw: a thirty foot pyramid with clusters of elliptical fruit highly prized by our early American settlers, most sought after for making a delicious rose-colored bread." What? You've never sought to bake a delicious rose-colored bread? You have no room in your garden for a thirty foot pyramid? Obviously it's time for you to change your lifestyle. You're thinking wrong.

"From South America where the gauchos roam the wild plains . . . [comes] silver pampas grass whose strong but delicate spikes can be dried for ethereally lovely arrangements to glamorize your interior throughout the winter months." Surely every chic interior should have this exotic touch. (Actually the description of this pampas grass sounds very much like a tall weed that grows along the Westchester parkways, that we always cut for its "ethereal" wheat colored plumes. They look so fine in umbrella stands.)

If you are still not tempted to fill out your order blank, the catalogue offers simple miracles: "Pomatoes": tomatoes above, potatoes below (the fine print reveals that this is two plants; sounds to me like both would starve); five kinds of roses on one bush—paint by numbers; five kinds of apples on one tree. . . .

Seed catalogues promise everything.

If some evil should crawl into your private Eden, valiant armies of lady bugs, earthworms, and praying mantises will be shipped express collect. You have your choice of egg cases that will hatch on arrival or chilled drowsy adults waiting to be galvanized by sunlight. Poison wands will sting crabgrass without singeing your lawn. Specially constructed weather vanes thump the ground and scare moles away. All bloom is guaranteed. Nothing can fail. Send back limp roots for complete refund. No green thumb necessary. You can have a lifetime of beauty for less than the cost of dinner and a show.

This is an offer too good to refuse.

Of course, all of us who are old hands know that these pages will never bloom in our gardens. How many asparagus roots, dehydrated strings of rhubarb, flakes of seed and corms of this and that have I planted, or rather *buried* in my backyard where empty packet markers stand like paper tombstones! "You planned a carpet of daylilies here," the sign says to me. "This was supposed to be a dazzling four foot tall hibiscus by July; it was supposed to be the focus of everyone's eye." "Here lie anemones, shades of Aphrodite's footsteps."

Where is the asparagus? This? This limp fern? "Cut when one inch thick," the catalogue instructed. Hah! This tattered spindle will never make it. Where are the perennial trillium, the lupine, the wild flowers with names right out of Ophelia's mad song? You'd think what can grow wild on its own would be doubly grateful for my solicitous planting, would spring out of the ground, bright as Easter. Not so. My good intentions lie dead and buried somewhere in the dappled sunlight of my backyard. And here am I. Poring over the new catalogues.

The March wind is blowing—gusts up to forty-eight miles an hour. The power company is concerned. I am pleased. I know the wind is busy drying the cold, drenched soil, making it friable so that the dark clods will flake through my fingers and I will feel that I am handling the primordial stuff of life, that I am a participant in paradise.

I won't grieve over April showers. The straight heavy rains must seep through the newly aerated soil as the May sun, dawdling but inevitable, warms the sleeping seed, sprouting dreams. Water-hungry roots will thread; leaves, spun tentatively out of stems, weave light into green silk.

I know the snowdrop that blooms before people venture out. Shy snowdrop, head hung like a bell that is too shy to chime the changing year. . . . This first flower is still the color of snow, as though winter too wants a hand in sculpting spring; lacking the gaudy palette of April, it does the best it can. Crocuses rush up, tawdry purple and yellow like lollipop wrappers. Violets get ideas. You have to hurry to find the winter flowers. If the weather is too cold and bleak, you may never see them. In March the orchestra enters the pit and begins to tune the instruments. You may hear a fiddle random as a crocus, or a brief scale on a flute. You have to listen close.

And then—lights on! In a spendthrift shower of gold, forsythia nets the sunlight. The show begins: sarabande of unfurling leaves, burgeoning nubs of dogwood and quince, pussy willow (missing link? furred flower), the heavy scent of hyacinth and lilac and paper-white narcissus, flowers, flowers everywhere: cool, tinted motels for travelling bees.

Really—only the shadow of truth lies in the gaudy pages of the seed catalogues. No prose could be flowery enough to convey the miracle that governs the heart-cracking unfolding of a rosebud into a pirouetting ballerina, that hooks blind claws of morning glories to any upward line, that turns spent flowers into new seeds and old stems into new earth.

We gardeners know you don't need a forest of eight-inch technicolor blooms. It is not necessary to "be the envy of your friends" or the "focus of all eyes." We can count on a far richer harvest. We have only to watch and read the lessons in the garden. Shakespeare writes in *As You Like It* of men and women who forego the intrigues of court life to take to the forest where they find "books in running brooks and sermons in stones." Whitman writes of "Leaves of Grass," and I always ask my students what he meant by that title. By "Leaves" I think he meant "leaves" of a book, because Whitman, following Emerson and Thoreau, believed that the true word of God was corrupted by too much dependence upon a rote reading of texts. Our word "book" indeed, comes from the Anglo-Saxon "bok" or beech-tree, because books were originally carved on the smooth bark of the beech. So the analogy even makes literal sense.

So what does it say in a garden? Like any book, the message is a joint product of the author and the reader. I ask my students what they think Whitman may have meant by grass; that is, what are the qualities of grass that Whitman may have meant to emphasize?

"It grows everywhere," they say, "on parks and lawns and cemeteries."

"It is sturdy."

"Even after it browns from frost or severe drought it comes back green at the first hint of warm rain."

"The more you cut it, the more you have."

"It's plain."

"It's cheap."

And what is it like?

"Like people," they say.

And I agree, "Grass is simple and straight and everywhere, resilient and durable as people."

When I look at my garden, when I read it, I see four great books: Change, Hope, Patience, Vitality. Success, it says, comes often when and where you least expect it. Life is the one principle that prevails. Don't give up: who of us—trained to value appearance and instant achievement as we are—could see the possibility in anything so drab and unassuming as a seed? And who made that complicated genetic program so compact? The giant computers that are wired to the little computer in my son Tom's barn can't begin to match the complicated set of responses and metamorphoses in a single seed. There is far too much coordinated order, too much flamboyant creativity to accept chance as First Cause. What is the reason for the variations upon the theme of butterfly? The intricately designed night-spun spider web traps the morning dew and sets a sweet morning breakfast table for the spider's prey. But Who designed the spider?

Every petal, every branch plainly bears God's signature. Perhaps that's why we garden on our knees.

It's not easy in the green world. We learn that too. The struggle is fierce. Nature shows little compassion. I doubt that the mole tunnels to ease the path for the root. Zinnias are not willing sacrifices to Japanese beetles, nor do the beetles scuttle joyously to the jaws of the praying mantis. Early worms are always in trouble. But it all seems to form one picture: Life is All. Each death is a tribute to eternity. A cycle is, by definition, eternal. The best survive and transmit their characteristics to the next generation and the strategies of survival are unlimited.

Perhaps the very variety of adaptation is another lesson. Things are tough? Cope. Old ways don't work? Try new ones. Fatten your leaves and store your own like a cactus if water is in short supply. In other words, enlarge your receptors so that you can practice emotional thrift; be your own cistern. Bees bothering you? Grow thorns. Wind topples you? Grow roots out of trampled stem. They can't keep a good plant down.

The list, of course, is infinite. And infinity is another miracle. How can the basic trinity of root and stem and leaf appear in so many guises? And disguises? Does it tell us to adapt, to change, to keep only what works? Flowers are, by nature, pragmatic.

"Hope. Chin up," the garden seems to say. How else could it survive in pelting rain and scorching sun? Fight through weeds and dogs? Nothing can keep a good stem down. With luck and a little care most plants will rally, even after a drought or an inundation of weeds. There is nothing so amazing as the recovery of a woe-begone leaf: one day limp as despair, the next stiff as a flag in the wind. It is as though the will not only to health, but to *flowering*, splendid health, were the ascendant drive.

A child plays garden by sticking bits of leaf and stem and carrot top into the ground. So simple. Yet oddly enough, it works. "Be fruitful and multiply" is the command. Given the natural inexhaustibles of sun and rain, any caprice seems to serve germination. And further, it seems that, once in bloom, flowers want to be picked. A garden is a generous place. The more blooms you cut, the more you have. Ignore your plants and they will sadly brown and go to seed. Could there be a parallel intended between this and human capacities? Could the garden be saying to the gardener: "Aptitudes sharpen through use, wither when neglected."

When I go out into the garden and put my hands on the warm dirt, something stirs, as though we were exchanging greetings. A new connection forms and the petty restrictive order of the hours I give to Caesar, fades away. My fingers decode weeds from seedlings. With little effort on my part, the whole parade from crocus through coreopsis to chrysanthemum will march across my garden assuring me of beauty even if the extravagant claims of the catalogue's new purchases do not bloom.

Were I blind I could find the raspberry jam scent of a climbing rose, the peppery tomato, the spicy marigold. I am familiar with the rasp of jay and cardinal, the wild crow call and the lonely doves who come to summer in my garden.

It is a good book—the one that is written in the garden. It says—dirt, yes! Work, yes! Sun on your back. Mist in your hair. Gray days are for planting. Light is not all. Patience.

Nothing lasts and nothing is lost. The only constant is change. The gardener is a key part, but by no means the ruler of the world. The driving ego is eased. We suffer no longer from total solitude nor total responsibility. Someone else is in charge. How many times, against a wall, no alternatives visible, has light suddenly appeared from a totally unexpected quarter? The catalogue is only a winter dividend, a rainbow-colored reminder of the promise of spring.

The year I forgot to order cosmos, they seeded themselves, tossed flat-petalled pink and purple heads simple as a child's crayoning. I have one cosmos that grows five feet tall and plants itself every year in its special corner of the garden, even though cosmos are supposed to be an annual.

Once I wished for a sunflower, and suddenly I had one. Then the birds ate all the seeds so swiftly it looked more like an unscraped dinnerplate than a flower. But of course this was one more way of reminding me of what every gardener knows: the plants are only mine to tend, not to own.

No planter works alone. Alienation is a product of the concrete, man-encrusted world. The wind that whips my willow blows my hair and sows my seed. We are comrades. Here is touch without fear. Once I had a student who was an aerial photographer in Vietnam and he said, "I liked the rain. Not only because it meant we would not have to fly, but because the rain touched me, and it didn't hurt." Rain was his only reminder of love.

The plot of the Artist is plain, the flyleaf is dedicated to beauty and to life. A flower is the triumph of the old seed and the cradle of the new. We are all partners in a slow green dance. Now you see it. Now you don't. Patience abets possibility. Hope grows high.

So I have failed. So perhaps half of the seeds I have planted have never come up. My garden is not the cynosure of all eyes, nor the envy of my neighbors. Quite the reverse as a matter of fact. "Your poppies only bloom for a few days?" my neighbors say, shaking their heads with that sympathetic glee one friend may feel for another's catastrophe. "They should last two weeks." Then I counter that poppies aren't worth the trouble if they're only going to last two weeks.

But now in March, I take stock. I think I'll order a sturdier rhubarb this year. Perhaps I planted last year's too deep. I'll set out one dwarf peach tree and that rose, "Peace," that Jackson and Perkins photograph so beautifully.

March wind howls through the empty trees and rattles my window panes and reaches down into the secret interstices of the earth and whispers to sleeping roots. "Wake up. Wake up. It's that time again. Hurry up, please. It's time."

I brood over the bright pages of the catalogues and order much more than I should. But the catalogue is only mailed to customers. A great bible, free for all to read, lies spread open, right there in every backyard.

# CITY SPRING

BANNERS of heralding robins unfurl in the equinoctial winds of March, summoning snowdrops from the earth and coral bells of quince. Blossoms, suddenly uncocooned, tremble like butterflies on the dogwood trees. In the softening earth of my garden I dig up old raspberry canes and overeager multiflora and teeter on a ladder sawing a mulberry trunk away from an apple tree before the leaves come to mask the intrusion.

The wind is bright blue and cold, freighted with the heavy musk of hyacinth and narcissus. Winter weeds mat among the sprouting bulbs. Crocuses still pop up in shady corners where hoops of violet are beginning to cluster. I always think, come about March, when I am as impatient as the flowers, eager to be up and see what comes next, I always think then: I could live no further south than New York because spring, being less missed, would be less welcome. And on the other hand, I could live no further north, because I couldn't bear to wait one more week.

I must see the signs by April: emperor tulips big as cups, hyacinths like chips of sky and daffodils sun-distilled, a child's garden of colors, poles apart on the color wheel. Nothing is further than yellow from red, than blue from yellow or red. Yet travelling from the most distant points of the spectrum brings the wheel ineluctably home: yellow leads through orange to red, then through purple to blue, and on through green to yellow again. Colors troop in orderly rows in the April kindergarten. The message is clear. The circle proclaims forever, world without end. A bluejay blooms in the apple tree as the nimble-fingered twigs spin petals in the dark.

But spring came to the city in a whoosh of litter blowing round corners, piling up in doorways. Pansies and geraniums appeared in supermarkets, and on Jane Street, Greenwich Village, Pam's part of Manhattan, the stone window boxes slowly filled. Curtains blew from open windows and ivy, newly wakened, gripped the red stone walls and climbed.

Spring clothes were featured in the fashionable boutiques, along with patchwork quilts and India prints and "thirties" dresses with mid-calf skirts and puffy sleeves. Everything is for sale in Manhattan. The city is a huge emporium: different products are sold in different sections. In the West Village they sell *avant garde* elegance. The prices are upper-middle-class high, but the merchandise pretends to an original cachet. In the 70's heavy Victorian is "in" (with an overlay of yoga): Tiffany glass, incense, copper washtubs, boxes of ugly beads, rickety wicker rockers, marble lamps. And then there are the health food shops where customers may mix their own tea leaves and coffee beans, and bearded young men in granny glasses and aprons pretend to be country storekeepers and gravely measure and weigh.

There are ice cream parlors and pancake shops and quasi-European espresso coffee houses, where rich blends of coffee, chocolate and whipped cream are served and poets may come and read their poems or young entertainers will stage their acts, while proprietors hover in the background and say they don't care for money at all. They just sell whatever it is they happen to be selling because they "love" their merchandise, sometimes can barely part with it.

Pam's New York was not my New York. It was a lonelier place . . . shadowed with questions.

All around the spring-softened elegant streets, the West Village flickers; there are glints of candlelight from expensive restaurants. Young men and women in tightfitting dungarees and flowered shirts stroll through the quiet streets together. Everywhere Pam looked there were pairs of young people walking through the streets, sometimes walking big heraldic dogs, sometimes with a child riding high on a backpack.

Pamela went to these restaurants, gazed across the romantically shadowed napery at—no one in particular (that is no one who turned out to "matter")—in those spring gardens where elegant cool pours off leaves and shaded stones as though dollar bills themselves cast a special cool verdure.

Sometimes the young men assumed romantic postures, but after a while they would earnestly tell involved tales of their troubles, their identity crises, their fears that what they were doing was not the precise assignment to bring them the blissful fulfillment they sought. These young men, Pam said, were exactly like the women at work, those who attend those consciousness-raising sessions where the air is dusty with doubt and despair.

She began asking herself if she was doing the wrong work. Perhaps publishing is really a paper tiger, removed from reality. She thought she'd try nursing. That was concrete. Why should she read about the treatment of a disease when she was trained to do something about it? How long, she asked herself, would she stay on the margins of life?

So she was hired as a nurse. Pam is good at getting jobs. Experienced personnel people seem to sense that there is something not quite adaptable about her. They seem to say, when she leaves, "I thought you wouldn't stay." They know she attends to some mysterious un-job-oriented compulsions. But I suppose total commitment is rare in employees these days. She plainly has an original intelligence, which, I suppose, is rare and the reason why case-hardened personnel people will take the gamble and hire her.

She went to work, and there was Mrs. Finklestein. Mrs. Finklestein was the patient in 409 who'd had a stroke. One-half of her body, from top to bottom, was inert, one eye closed, one leg limp. But the other side was all life. Mrs. Finklestein always begged to have her door left open so she could monitor the hospital corridor. She bragged about her husband and her life, but she had this bright blue eye and this gentle way with the nurses so that they actually liked coming to serve her.

And what did she say to Pamela? To Pamela she said, "Tell me, dearie, you married? . . . No? . . . Nice girl like you, not married? Mmmmmmm. Mmmmmmmm. . . . I'll find you someone. You know how all the doctors come in to see me. . . . I'll find you a nice young doctor. . . . (and then) . . . Pamela, dear, would you mind please to give me a little more back rub, there, down there, that's right. . . . You have great hands, dearie, great hands. . . . I'm not going to get you a doctor. No, Sir." Pamela paused in her ministrations and listened to the breathing hum of the hospital, the passing rubber wheeled carts, the low urgencies of the intercom: "inhalation therapist to cardio-vascular . . . inhalation therapist to . . ." There was always a flicker of uniforms like gulls in the corridor. Mrs. Finkelstein shut her one good eye and then opened it dramatically: "Do you know what I'm going to get for you?" she asked triumphantly. "No." "I'm going to get you a nice young *specialist!*"

Visitors to the man in 411 brought him bottles of whiskey hidden in their briefcases, even though the patient was dying of cirrhosis of the liver. But the sick man denied it: "Surrrre, I niver touch the stuff. It's me friends' bottles layin' around. Can't expect them to come visiting these hot spring nights with never a drop to ease their thirst now, can you, nurse? . . . You come around to my bar when I get out of here. It's not far. You come around and have a drink with me. Whaddya say, nurse?"

Another part of the job was the cold intercom-pitched voice of the nursing supervisor muttering "attitude, something about your attitude, Miss Evslin . . . the morning you forgot . . . the time you came late . . . the chart you didn't finish . . . the chart you spent too much time on . . . each girl must complete her care in time for the next shift."

Pam would dawdle home crosstown from the hospital. She liked to feel the wind in her uncapped curls. She liked mooning in shop windows, at her own face, her blue coat open and flapping in the wind, white stockings strange as stork legs, white rubber-soled shoes padding slowly past the quiet brownstones and the occasional shop windows of thirteenth street. She hated to walk down fourteenth street, past the winos and the open air markets with their shabby goods, plastic shoes, paper flowers and dust. But thirteenth was elegant and secret. She liked knowing her way about the city. She liked the other nurses and her patients in the hospital—and the supervisor? Who cares about supervisors on a fine spring day?

Once she found a beautiful old pedal sewing machine in a table for $25 in one of the second-hand stores. And another day, on the curb, she literally picked up a fine chair that was too delicate for anything but plants to sit on. The chair had a bird carved on its back. And then she bargained the sewing machine man into selling her two ladder-backed cane-seated chairs for $25. He did, as long as she agreed to take four volumes of Shakespeare for $30; the bindings were destroyed, but the print was excellent. Then she found a soft green cardigan waiting outside her incinerator which she gave to Bud, who loved it.

So she was quite free, my girl, my city-bird daughter in her eyrie high on a rock and steel and glass mountain, too high for pigeons but with a view of river-scouring gulls. She lived here with her white cat and the blue couch and the poster (a very rare Chagall print the storekeeper assured her, pocketing her $75) of a curly-haired clown with a crooked smile, who looked as if he might have been her brother. The poster hung under glass opposite her door. When she entered or left, the smile was always there, the eyes watching tenderly, blotting out the great vacant stare of the window, the indifferent sky, and the rosy lamplight view of people passing by the windows of other apartments, handing things to each other, and disappearing.

Fedora the white cat waited on the blue couch and she could hear him calling as she turned the key in the lock. The elevator door slammed and she noticed the mysterious look a room has when only one person lives in it. It is as though the room had been holding its breath: every cup, every shoe placed or misplaced, of course, exactly as she'd left it. Don't call, "Hello." Nobody's home. Pam held her cat in her arms. He was lost in the whiteness of her uniform. But he scrambled off her lap and ran howling to the kitchen. He was starved.

She poured milk into his dish and, because she was tired, her hand trembled and some of the milk spilled. She watched the milk run over the floor.

She had to get out. She went out on the Village streets, at least there were people there. She bought a pair of elegant dungarees, and then she wore them down to the cellar where she did her wash and spilled bleach on them. She spilled bleach on most of her clothes because nurse's uniforms take a lot of bleach, and when she walked past the doorman in her white-stained dungarees she felt more than ever like some visitor from outer space. Every other girl in New York seemed to be dressed in the height of original elegance (beads, tie-dyed, swish of peasant skirt, svelte tooled leather belts, manicured toenails and artfully criss-crossed leather sandals). Every girl in New York had shining golden hair, saxophone gold, that played as she walked, "See meeee! See meeee! See how I beautiful I am!" like a cadenza on a jazz saxophone. And every girl in New York had a boy to walk with, or was about to meet one. And then, of course, Pam had also walked with and dined with many young men, but it seemed to her they were so coated with the dust of the city that they were barely visible. Bread she ate with them was less than bread, soufflés sagged, ice cream melted. They took her to avant garde films in intimate chic theatres where the giant screens were full of matched profiles. Whispers bounced off the balcony walls. Crunch of popcorn underfoot when the films were finished and the audience filed through the smoke-filled lobbies and into the quiet spring night. The sound of the pavement against her platform soles said, "So what? So what? So what?"

But Pamela had a letter stuffed in her pocketbook. It was from a boy she hadn't seen for years although they'd been corresponding regularly. The letter said he was coming to New York. He wasn't sure exactly when, but it would be soon. He would come to New York and look her up.

"Maybe . . ." she thought.

# ANTHROPOLOGY IN THE MULTIFLORA

AT A PARTY late in spring, I met a man who has been running a successful dry-cleaning establishment for over twenty years. But he has another calling as well. Every day as he drives home from work he plans what he will make for the family dinner, shops for any special ingredients he may need, goes home, starts pots simmering. Then he steps out into his backyard to pick the chard, leeks, yellow tomatoes, cardoons—whatever he needs.

He is an expert catalogue gardener. All the exotica that I fail at, he does magnificently. He was even featured once in *The New York Times* garden section. The picture showed him coming home from work and stepping out into his backyard—not to flop on a lawnchair, but to tie tomatoes, to search and destroy wild morning glories. This was his way of resting from his labors in the office. He had dug up his whole backyard, and, instead of wrestling with crabgrass and lawnmower, he was harvesting his tiny farm. "Cantaloupe, so big!" he boasted. "Leeks, braised in butter. Never cook without plenty of leeks and butter."

We exchanged recipes. Bud fancies himself a gourmet cook too and he chimed in. Suddenly the whole idle chit-chat of a room full of strangers became focused. We were not name-dropping, we were vegetable-dropping. The plants had become the totemic figures in our lives. A touch of leaf bestowed more excitement than some third-hand encounter with those official "People" who appear in magazines, or the numbers that chime like bells through so many conversations. I remember a man who told me that his son was marrying a girl whose father had a farm of two thousand acres, with two hundred cows and twelve tractors. I know you can't handle two thousand acres without tractors, but the emphasis seems wrong. I pictured the acres stacked high-rise style, heard cows ping like cash registers, and the tractors droned like monster bees.

But my part-time-farmer dry-cleaner really seemed to be "into" his land. You rarely meet someone at a party who communicates a sincere feeling the way this man did, a sincere *positive* feeling.

So, come Sunday I went out into my backyard and analyzed the situation. A good ten-foot border along the south-west was a tangle of multiflora and mulberry and wild raspberry. This would be our farm. We were not about to dig up the whole backyard. We need room for grandchildren to play, but ten by fifty was a good patch for beginners, we thought. So the battle with the brambles was launched.

You can't even compost multiflora; it would be too painful to recycle. The thorny canes had to be stuffed into spare trashcans and old plastic bags. I don't buy plastic bags by the package because I've heard that the sea is becoming salted with little indissoluble pieces of waste plastic. Sea and earth will not accept a tampered molecular structure. There's something beautiful and perhaps important about that. Perhaps it is a way of telling us that our success with synthetics is really a failure. When something is inadmissible to the great regenerative cycle, are we playing with forbidden fruit? Will we be driven out of our final garden? Do we disobey natural warnings at our peril?

The trouble with writing about gardening is that so much is written in that backyard that one tends to go off on tangents. But the glory of working in the backyard is that nothing stops you from thinking as your hands are busy.

So there I was, carefully placing the cut multiflora canes vertically like umbrellas so they wouldn't tangle in each other's hair and block compacting. I had to wear heavy jacket and gloves like a bee-keeper. I had to work fast before the new spring growth would come to thicken the tangle.

A guest, out from the city, said, "Why don't you get a gardener to clean all that mess? Why don't you get a gardener to put your place in shape?"

Then why have a garden at all? Just to look at? That's only the end product. And end products come so quickly: flip a channel, hop a plane, dial a prayer. So we plunder ourselves with our own greed. We value nothing but results. The more removed a person is from the production of the results that fill his days, the more we esteem him. He is a "rich" man, we say, because he can afford to hire laborers.

But you might also say he is a poor man. His pockets may be full, but his hands are empty, his strength unused. He doesn't "know" his garden, and he doesn't "know" the aptitudes of his own body. One of the charges levied against the housewife is that she doesn't use her "mind," her formal education if she's had one. Sons of gardeners and contractors come to our college to "upgrade" themselves, to get the prestigious white-collar high-paying jobs.

I've nothing against college. But I don't think it is the

only place for an education. Too many students go through unscathed by a single thought. White collar jobs are not always interesting, often bring ulcers and other manifestations of nervous fatigue simply from confinement to a desk and four walls, and the white collar job does not always pay as well as work in some unionized industry.

Perhaps it is the separation I am inveighing against, dividing our lives, placing artificial limits on alternatives, judging, grading. Why should office skills be considered "Up" while hand skills are considered "Down"? Why should it be more prestigious to move around papers than to move around mops and plants? And, more important, why should anyone's life be devoted exclusively to using his or her mind *or* body? Why not use both? When we *save time* by hiring labor, are we losing time we could spend improving our own bodies, our physical skills?

We are a very sports-minded country, yet more and more of our appetite for sports is satisfied by an eye-straining television set with a bowl full of peanuts and a six pack of beer. Our adrenalin pumps immediately to meet the opponents' challenge, but our limbs rest in a recliner.

But outside in the garden the weeds launch a vigorous offensive. Branches toss evil shadows over vegetable gardens, pipes leak, timbers sag and rot, leaves clog rain gutters, and the grass races after the lawnmower. This could sound like a pesky list of handyman chores or like a great contest. It depends how you look at it. It is either the nuisance or the challenge of life in an old house in the suburbs.

For me it's a challenge, and I enjoy that.

So armed with a wicked pair of clippers, I attacked the

multiflora and stuffed it into trashcans. The growth was so dense it was hard to detect any progress at first. But that was part of the fun. Then I found the timbers of an old canoe we had drydocked one winter and, in our sailing enthusiasm, never re-launched. That's how thick the growth was, covering a whole canoe. I found peonies trying to be. I found the apple tree had reached one branch down into the earth as though it were trying to root in a new spot. The branch must have anchored. I didn't want to disturb it and prod, but a new apple twig was growing straight up out of the ground as though it had every intention of becoming a new tree.

I found a lot of mulberries that thought they might as well be a forest too, crowding among the ailanthus that had the same idea. I found a tiny rubber thong sandal that must have belonged to one of my children. And suddenly I was an anthropologist on the track of a lost civilization. But it was not a stranger's roots I was excavating, but my own.

Whose sandal? Who came out here to pick raspberries, perhaps, wandering further and further among the thorny thickets, lost a shoe and came limping in to the soft grass? I see a small child in summer. (Boy or girl? I don't know. Thongs are unisex. But they are summer shoes.) It must have belonged to one of the girls because this is a very tiny thong, small as they make them, and Tom was nine and Bill was five when we moved here.

Guessing further, I can postulate a browned shoulder, that exquisite round before muscles harden, slightly damp with summer heat and that particular fragrance of sun on damp grass and a little dirt that clings to children who play in gardens. I used to love to take pictures of my children when they were smaller than the cosmos. I would let them creep, just to pose them; they wandered with the cat in a marigold jungle.

What does a small girl think as she voyages in her own backyard? Safe, I should imagine. Dog and cat and squirrel pose no threat. Bushes make good parlors for tea parties; apple blossom petals are served on flat stones. There is a special magic to being in spy position, out of sight of adult eyes, being able to hide where the huge can't follow. If one is very still, a robin may hop close, or a squirrel. Our robins are so bold they chase the jays away. A small child might enjoy that rout. Cheeky, that's what robins are.

And I can remember even further back in time to those soft cloth books with wide-eyed birds and wide-skirted little girls illustrating Mother Goose rhymes. I remember a favorite: "The north wind shall blow, and we shall have snow . . . And what will poor robin do then? He'll hide in the barn and keep himself warm, and tuck his head *under* his wing, poor thing." At which point the listening child would raise a stubby arm to cover face and close eyes, pretending sleep. The rhythm is cosy as rain.

Twenty years later when I became a teacher, I heard about learning disabilities. I heard about children so neglected they didn't know the meaning of "under" or "over." Apparently this not only fouls their depth perceptions, but also impairs their ability to conceptualize abstractions . . . to say the least. And I also learned in education courses that this gap in early teaching can never be mended. The only barely encouraging results have been on a one-to-one tutorial level. And then I wonder why it is more prestigious to be a teacher of strangers than the mother/teacher of your own flesh and blood.

You never realize, when you're mothering, what little things will matter terribly in the years to come. But I'm glad the memory of my children's childhood belongs to me, that I did not entrust them to strangers.

When Janet comes to visit, I'll show her the sandal and tell her that it was hers and she will grow tender and misty-eyed as she always does when I speak of her own past. And then, for a lark, I'll tell Pam when she comes that I found her sandal in the bushes. She won't care at all. Pam is more interested in the future than in the past.

So there I was—clipping and tying and dreaming in my private jungle—a lovely constructive calisthenic complete with huffing and puffing (deep breathing) after a week of pacing around stuffy classrooms. And there among the multiflora I studied my anthropology. True, I found no Algonquin arrowheads, no Pleistocene artifacts, although I wouldn't recognize them if I did. I've seen exhibits of Westchester arrowheads that closely resemble the stones in my garden.

But I did find artifacts of early Evslin. Holding a small familiar shoe is another way of getting back to the magic circle, another way of certifying my past. Yes, it says, these fine young women who come and go when they visit your front porch, these fine young women were once your children. And I can imagine the day when Tanya, Bill's daughter, will come with tiny yellow thongs, and she will try to climb the fence that separates my vegetable garden from the lawn. And she will complain that her shoe is caught in the fence, that she can't get over.

And she will not see, of course, until she is a grandmother (My! How far the generations whirl!) how the present is also the past, how the pictures are always there to flicker like a deck of picture cards. Memory is just like the primitive animation we played with in elementary school holding a deck of picture cards, and flipping through the deck to make a horse jump over a fence. Later we'd put a penny in the stereopticon that stood outside the candy store. Crouched over the eyepiece, we could watch men and women walking jerkily through doorways as the still pictures flipped. We could drop our pennies in over and over and see the same actions repeated. It was hard to believe there were no tiny men and women inside the machine flashing through the doorways and waltzing down the streets.

Just so do the pictures of my children and my children's children live in the stereopticon of memory, flashing on and off, in and out. They are forever young, caught like the tableau in Keats' "Ode to a Grecian Urn." I cannot write an ode and I cannot paint a picture. But digging in a back-yard tangle, I've unearthed a private artifact, a talisman of a civilization that is completely inconsequential to the rest of the world, and of absolutely bedrock significance to me.

So I wonder, as I reach high from my ladder to yank the web of vine that has been strangling the apple tree for so long, that I never really knew the tree was there until I saw one flowering branch last year, just one, and a heap of bitter apples tumbled in the grass. This tree is a gift, I thought. Thank You for the gift, so many gifts (how many?) which stand quietly in their wrappings.

But there is thanks for much more than the tree. Standing, supposedly mindless on the ladder, not using (?) my college education, not getting paid, not doing any work I could proclaim to the world so that it (the world) would know and applaud me, I was not only a gymnast and a horticulturist, but a sociologist, a cultural historian, the history no less significant because of its private nature.

Two girls once attended a "women's studies" seminar I conducted. One girl was blooming and attractive, but she was unhappy. "I have two children, and I love them very much and I love my husband. But I don't feel that I am doing enough," she said. The other girl had a haggard face, but her voice was strong, very strong. "I'm a sociologist," she said, "I study family relationships." I said, "You mean your work is to knock on this mother's door and see what she's doing?"

"Ye-es."

"Surely, then, if a mother's work is worth studying, it must be worth doing."

There is no learning of the *new,* Plato says, but only a recognition of buried perceptions. When we learn something we say—oh yes, that is the way it should be, or, that explains what I've always wondered about, or, yes, I can swivel my frame of reference to comprehend that.

So, the little shoe brings me the buried years, the compost of memory, and, applying it to Tanya—since this is such a practical world and all knowledge must be applied —I can see the tentative testing gaze of her father in her eyes, and I can see that she is not my son come again, but a part of my son and a part of her mother, all composted into that delightful amalgam of a little new girl, Tanya.

I understand her curious, bold, delicate gesture as she catches her shoe in my garden fence. She cannot walk in the wild tangle where my little girls walked, because I've changed my emphasis now. I'm growing tomatoes and peppers where once I grew children. But I have time to sit and accept pebbles from her, one by one. I have more time now. "Please," I say. "Peeeze," she says, and her voice is very soft as she mimics mine.

You don't get far from children around here, thank God. One group goes and sends back these tiny emissaries.

All that blustery March and into April I battled the multiflora and the wild mulberries and the ailanthus. Bud baled them and we put them out for the trash, but the Queen City Refuse Company only allows five bundles a week, so for a long time our curb looked like the thorned hedge around Sleeping Beauty's castle. I found it rather pleasant to be surrounded by a storybook wall.

Then we ordered one of those newspaper ads—thirty-two hemlocks for six dollars—"fastest growing hedge . . . complete privacy all year 'round." The fragrant bundle came like a sack of Christmas greens: "Plant with a handful of peat moss and evergreen fertilizer." Bud digs the holes. He's more careful than I am. He has a better planting record. The trees were no bigger than toddlers. He had to plant quickly before the roots dried. It really looked like a toy hedge, those childsized trees, as though we were sticking branches in the ground the way children play at gardening.

Most of the hemlocks lived, put forth bright green fingertips and prepared to meet one another's branches—four, five, six years from now—when they're big enough to stand arm in arm like a true hedge.

Digging, we found two old trowels with their centers oxidized away, trowel skeletons. This teaches us about rust and weather and what happens to iron when it is exposed to soft earth and gentle rain (science) and why we always have to buy new trowels (husbandry).

And then there was the morning we both woke up itching horribly. Digging in our bramble jungle, we must have come across a patch of poison ivy.

# MOVING DAYS

THE PHONE RANG.

It was Pam.

"I'm moving," she said. "I found the most marvelous apartment. Only $180 a month. It has a brick wall and a fireplace . . . and a big kitchen and . . . not really a bathroom . . . that is, there is but you have to use the kitchen sink. No tub, but there is a shower . . . but not in the bathroom. . . . Now, mother, don't get so upset. A shower doesn't have to be in the bathroom. . . . No, really it doesn't. . . . I have a shower. I'll be clean. . . . I'll take my clothes to the laundromat. . . . That's not so far away. . . . I don't know. . . . not far. . . . Mother, please don't be so negative. . . . The shower? It's in the kitchen."

All right. I won't be negative. She's moving. She's the one who'll have to take the shower in the kitchen. If she doesn't mind, why should I? I'll concentrate on the brick wall and the fireplace. I don't believe parents should be negative. We don't know it all, and we certainly can't teach it all. Most real learning is what they call "Self-Instructional," do-it-yourself. Families can only love—which does not mean a permissive wash. But negatives should be reserved for crises or they simply serve as communication stoppers, and that's the end of that.

But why is it proving to be so difficult getting this last child settled? I don't know.

So I went to help Pam move out of Jane Street, and Bud joined me later because a man's hand is indispensable for tying knots. And we packed up all her pretty glasses and the other accretions of her visit to the Village. I took a sack of her winter clothes home for the dry cleaner. I remember the air conditioner was going and a fan. The windows were bare. She'd never bought curtains, but with all that sky and sun and stone out there, there was charm in the free view. Pam had put up a wild jungle wallpaper of lions and tigers with gay circus faces on a blue background. The next tenant was happy with the wallpaper, so it didn't have to be removed. The pattern was so much Pam, whose favorite toy had been a charming little Steif lion who could turn his soft wool head quizzically.

The phonograph whirred drowsily.

"I hate the doormen," she said. "I hate the way doormen are always minding other people's business." We rode down in the elevator, carrying the immigrant bundles of things we were taking home with us, and the vulpine well-dressed young men in the elevator looked down their long, long noses. Dark portraits glimmered in the lobby. The doorman smiled. He wasn't such a bad lot. Perhaps it was the image of authority.

You could feel a hint of summer in the dusky streets as the pavement began to warm. The kids were out playing stickball after supper. Dog-walkers passed, anchored like tents to the slant leashes of eager dogs. A sleepy garage attendant pointed out our car. We have this red Volvo that has hopped around everywhere with us for the past 120,000 miles. I wanted to paste a little "one" up on the mileage indicator because it doesn't register more than five digits. I love the old things in my life. And the young people.

There Pam stood, her bleach-stained dungarees eerie in the dark garage. She was due at work in the morning, button-bright. I could see her sleep-walking through the dawn streets, spillable pocketbook crammed too full. It's a miracle how she always got the medicine in the right vial, arm, tube. . . . Glimmer of girl in the dark garage. . . . Godspeed on your next move.

Maybe the new apartment would be great. If I had to live in New York, I think I would certainly stay in the West Village, no matter what the rent. I like the elegance, the shops and the restaurants, the reasonably clean streets and clean pedestrians. But I am not Pam. Her friends live in the lofts over on the East Side. She was moving nearer them, nearer to the hospital where she worked. Made some sense.

" 'By, love."

" 'By." Soft face lifted for a kiss.

And then she was "at home" at 250 Elizabeth Street and it was our turn to visit her there. After the swank stone castles on the East River Drive, we turned into Houston Street where garbage and people piled on the spring night curb and all the stores dropped steel walls in front of them to keep out night marauders. Negotiating Elizabeth Street and finding a parking space was a bit difficult. But we managed. Then it began to rain buckets, so we hailed a cab.

The cabbie must've thought we were provincials down sight-seeing, and that he'd have a nice long journey to our home or hotel. He couldn't believe it when we said "Elizabeth Street." He couldn't believe we'd want to stop and leave his cab anywhere around there—so hard for him to believe it that he drove right past 250, Pam's house. We had to stop him. Reluctantly, he let us go. The rain had abated slightly. We walked to 250.

Like Jane Street, Elizabeth Street is only a few blocks long, but it is much narrower. It's been a slum for as long as I can remember, lined with what are called "taxpayers," tiers of apartments built over stores. People hang out the windows, fat women in black dresses, men quietly smoking. A pile of small children were at work on the sand pit of a construction site. About one hundred feet before Pam's house stood what may have once been a store, a building with a huge plate glass front. The glass was missing now, and the opened front had the appearance of a stage. I looked in.

Upward, in the gutted interior, I saw a rope hanging with a knot at the end of it. As I watched, a pair of men's shoes appeared, then the lower half of a man's body, swinging slowly like a chandelier. Shoes, dungarees, a torn shirt— lower and lower the figure descended and more was visible, a pair of strong black arms holding on to the rope, and finally I saw the face of a young coal-black Tarzan who completed his descent, leaped off the rope, and vanished into the night.

There was a sofa sitting out on the sidewalk in front of this building; it was a red living room sofa.

I could have collapsed on it.

But there was a tattered old man asleep on this sofa. He was covered with soaking spreadout pieces of cardboard boxes. What was left of the rain scurried down the gutters, carrying cigarette butts and beer can keys.

I wished I could disappear down the rain gutter too and

swim out to the open sea. And I wished I could take my daughter with me. But she was twenty-five years old, self-supporting, not to order around.

But I will not describe the scent of the staircase in 250 Elizabeth Street where my daughter, the free woman, lived. I will not tell you that one of the doors to her apartment had a sheet of steel hammered to it like a prison, that her apartment had many doors, and that not all of them had locks. She had two fire escapes, one front and one rear, which, she explained, gave great cross-ventilation. True. To a mother's eyes, these fire escapes allowed complete freedom of entry and exit for any acrobatic marauders. They didn't even have to be Tarzans. Who can't climb a fire escape? I pointed this out to her.

"Yes. I know. I'm going to get a grill for the windows," she said, "but look, look at the marvelous view!" Indeed. From the front you could see all the tenants of Elizabeth street hanging out their windows, from the rear some limp shirts and a few weeds blooming in the courtyard. "In the summer they have a garden down there, and Fedora can go out and play."

She showed us the fireplace, a four inch recess in the brick wall where someone had tried to burn a cigarette package. She showed us the ladder to the high platform bed and an extra room that the tenant before her had partitioned. She'd purchased these "improvements" for $200. So now, instead of having a fifty-foot expanse from window to window, her apartment was broken up by one windowless room in the middle. This would be her dressing room, she explained gravely, because here everyone on the block was like one family and she was determined to be careful of her appearance.

"Yes, really, mother, it's true. When I first moved in, I went down to this grocery store and they said, 'You the nurse who's just moved in to 250? Hey, Joe, come and meet the nurse who's just moved. She lives in your building.' And Joe, I guess he's the son, comes out to meet me . . . just like a family. They watch you, not snooty like the doormen, but you're part of their block, you know. . . ."

"It's Mafia. All Mafia. . . . Did you notice the Italian groceries? (I did.) Well, it's all Mafia. Did you notice the Cadillacs. (I did.) They do their own patrol. Everything will be all right. . . ."

"Who's that singing around the corner?"

"Oh, that's just the Puerto Rican Social Club."

"I see. And who's that sleeping out on the sofa in the rain?"

"Him?"

"Yes."

"Oh, he's just one of the winos. They don't hurt anybody. Sometimes they put their foot out and try to trip you, but they're harmless. They're too far gone to cause any trouble."

"Of course. And the black man swinging from the rope?" I asked.

"Him?"

"Him."

"You saw him already? (She sputtered with laughter, but I don't think even she appreciated the joke.) He's a character!"

"Yes, I should imagine he is."

"Would you like some coffee?" she said brightly, turning towards her ice-box, setting out bread and cheese on her pretty plates.

"Pamela, would you like me to lend you the money to make another move? People make mistakes. . . ."

"Mother, please. I *like* it here. Wait'll you see; it's going to be beautiful. *Doesn't* it have a mar*velll*ous smell? A sculptor lived here before, the one who rented to me. Don't you think it smells like baking bread?" (Flour and water and old Plaster of Paris, and a white floury dust in all the cracks of the floorboards). "See how big the windows are?" (They were. Big as doors.) "See what a great breeze?" (There was.) "I'm going to put geraniums on the balconies and Fedora has found a friend, a great pirate cat with one ear chewed off. . . ."

"Well, as long as Fedora has such nice friends, what do I have to worry about?"

Yet we lived in a place not unlike Pam's in Georgia. I shouldn't forget that. I shouldn't be so suburban-spoiled that I think happiness depends upon plumbing. But I do know it depends upon—I think—the pronoun "we." Nonsense, a free girl doesn't have to be a "we" girl these days. I'm showing my true colors. I'm a square. Feminists are correct when they say I am "locked into the couples syndrome." The new freedom says a girl should not be considered a failure because she has not married, and that sounds like a charitable maxim.

But I know that when Bud and I were young and we battled roaches or whitewashed our privy or built bureaus out of cartons and tried to make an ice box out of a bag of rockwool insulation, there was a romance to it. Love was our private wall-to-wall luxury. The rest was the world's obstacle course. "These present woes will serve as sweet discourse in times to come," Bud used to say, quoting Shakespeare. He meant, don't worry that it's tough today.

Don't bug me about that. Some day we'll look back on this period fondly. He was right; we do!

Of course there's no point in being cruel and scorning the loners. But I wonder if it is helpful to tell a girl or a boy that mating is not an important part of life. Like everything else worthwhile, love and marriage often require some active searching. One has to take matters in hand and go a-courting. But, if you've been taught that love and marriage are not such desirable goals, opportunities may pass by. And then it is too late. Biology doesn't hold still. The loneliness of the empty middle years is a poor reward for the fierce "freedoms" of youth.

"But this is only *your* opinion," I've been told.

No. Men and women were made to be fruitful and multiply. That is my observation, but hardly my edict. The Lord's instructions to Noah were explicit about the necessity for couples. Otherwise all life would have disappeared.

"My goodness, Mother, all you can think about is guys. I have plenty of dates. I'll manage. There are other things in the world besides marriage. Look at all the divorces. Look at all the unhappy people screaming in the suburbs. (I've never met them, although I have read about them.) I'm going to make a life for myself. Just you watch. I'm going to make a great life for myself."

"Of course you will, pet."

We never uttered those words aloud, but we both heard them, loud and clear.

Pamela walked us around her new neighborhood. The winos stuck out their feet and leered stupidly, but they did not look capable of much damage. The singing from the Puerto Rican Social Club seemed to be a day and night affair. We found a Chinese laundry behind a grating two blocks away. Pam could wheel her wash here. There were millions of stores selling pieces of broken furniture, second hand shoes, chipped dishes, rare cheeses, plumbing equipment, headstones . . . everything she might possibly need. Downstairs, below her apartment, there was even a friendly butcher with a very friendly German Shepherd. And how did he show his friendship? Every time she came in the store, he said, "Good morning."

I noticed that the faces at the windows never changed: an old man with an unlit cigar, ladies huge as caryatids, resting on their mighty arms, staring, staring out the windows. Dirty-faced children scrabbling among the ashcans in the sandpile of the urban renewal project.

And there's Chinatown. Yes. Mott and Mulberry Streets with dragons on the lampposts and desiccated ducks hanging by their necks, fringes of noodles, smaller people going about their business in a great rush, tourist shops jingling . . . exotica, exotica . . . the many-fingered city . . . espresso palaces . . . Italian cakes larded with pink and green icing. ("Poison," my mother used to say, "poison." Vendors used to come with little carts selling cupcakes of whipped cream —charlotte russe. With poor refrigeration, they probably were poison. How long have mothers been despairing over their daughters' safety? Forever?)

Wise cabbies drove past . . . and pushcarts . . . and those strange men and women who recognize one another, to whom garbage is a garden and pushcarts bloom . . . men and women hailing each other, exchanging a knowing glance. I know I've seen too many movies, read too many books about the city. . . .

Elizabeth Street seems to be the underside where all the

strangeness shows, like the underside of a beetle.

Pamela took me to an Indian restaurant. Each wave of immigrants has come straight off the pier laden with groceries and recipes. And so many of them unpacked and went straight into the restaurant business.

We sat in a pitchdark Indian restaurant and ate flat crisp bread and hot spices and chutney and waiters the exact color of shadow glided to our table and spoke softly (as shadows) and left. And there was my girl in a big-brimmed hat that shadowed her pale brow, her eyes serious, a bit fatigued. "You know, Mother, I don't see anything too great about marriage. These boys I know, they're nice on a date, but I'm glad to be rid of them and be alone. . . ."

Back in our less artful suburbs, the golf course has turned bright green like those children's coloring sets where you paint with only water and the secret tints appear. Now the geese have to share the fairway and the waterhole with the golfers. At least once every spring the old rivers—who dug the first roadbeds where my car winds each morning—these old rivers rise to have a look at the cars. When the heavy rain coincides with high tides, the estuarial streams rise excitedly, run across the roads, flooding so deeply that cars send great fans of spray at each other as though they were suddenly water-winged. Then cars drown. Traffic slows.

I love that. Just as the autumn sun blinds our westering windshields, so do the spring floods hinder us. I love to see a whole flock of commuters (me included) who were dedicated only to getting there ahead of the next fellow, suddenly stopped by the river. "What river?" they say. "We never saw a river here."

Faith, someone said, is belief without evidence. Like Job, who believed in spite of the evidence. On the other hand, a materialist will say it is foolish to believe without evidence, that such faith is really superstition, invalid. "Validate" is the great word in scientific circles. It is the cousin of "Accountability," the fashionable maxim of the social sciences.

What *is* electricity? Or nuclear explosion? Or radioactivity? Are they not the fruit of the hypotheses of observing men who said, when faced with a manifestation of power without evidence of visible causation: "There must be something at work here. But I must set up new conditions for discovery. I need new tools, new forms, new vocabularies to validate what no one has *yet* seen." Do not the very roots of our material existence stem from the intuitive faith of a few men who have developed new means of detecting evidence?

I think there is more than surface cause and effect in my garden. I think what we do *not* see is as important as what we do see. A bird could look down and know where the bugs have gone or where a worm will emerge. Aphids cluster on the underbellies of leaves, and ants follow the trail of the aphids and milk the tiny herd. Roots pause to brood over stones. Trinka, our dog, knows the low fence is to keep her out. When she is in an honorable mood, or thinks someone is watching, she respects the fence. But all these are food-motivated aptitudes, measured by calculators I do not possess.

Man, I think, was given the gift of vision beyond food

and sex. That's what the evolutionists cannot explain—that's the great difference, between man and all animals.

For instance, mornings as I pass the lake on my way to school, I see where the driftwood lies like buried treasure and the grey branches of overhanging trees have fallen, plop, into the water and lie there. Writhing? No. Only insofar as the water moves. The branches lie there almost still, water buried, water-lit, saying, "See me. Search me. Dive into this gray brackish pool and fetch what was never there."

Branches poise on tree trunks. They stare, demure, "It is not our fault that you are an image-seeker," they say. "It is not our fault that you have suddenly glimpsed a palisade of sunken tree. It is not our fault that the peculiar angle of morning sun and this stillness before the wind scrubs—or veils—the face of the water has allowed you to see what was never there."

Or was it there? If I see it, it exists for me. To stretch Descartes: "I see, therefore I am." That I know with the part of my mind that remembers: do not touch a hot stove . . . do not step into an open hole . . . that part of my mind that calculates in prose and can postulate danger from the innocent aspects of things.

So I know that a tree is a fine enough creature in itself, a dead tree barbed against the morning sky. But, drown a tree and watch it swim in the green embrace of its fellows. Then I dive for the treasure my eyes have sunk and grapple it to me with hooks of memory.

Fish swim through the buried branches. A duck paddles, on the prowl. They do not see my trove of trees. They lack the calibrating equipment; they are not interested in measuring visions.

But, perhaps, faith is easy in the suburbs. It grows in gardens, feeds on sunlight. What happens on Elizabeth Street?

Pam worked hard on her apartment—spring cleaning. Spring, summer, fall—the first cleaning it ever had, I'll bet. She scrubbed down the crumbling brick wall and tried to seal it with a kind of brick varnish that the dessicated stones sucked up and, parched as ever, demanded more. She scrubbed the old stained floor with Mex and a stiff brush and rubber gloves. She set geraniums out on the window sills. We spoke about gratings for the windows. Yes, of course, she would, she would. One-quarter of the apartment was kitchen (if you forget that it was also shower room). The two big windows and the wooden floor and the round table had a rustic calendar charm. She hung bright plates up. Pam had a way with places.

She worked all day in the hospital and then came home and worked on her apartment so that by nightfall she fell asleep in almost a swoon of exhaustion.

Then, one night, as she lay in bed, the geranium pot fell off the window sill. The sound reverberated in the corridors of her sleep like a gunshot. Her eyes opened, pulling her into the darkness, forcing her awake. She knew something had entered the apartment. There was that stillness she remembered well from her childhood on the water, when all the winds seem to center, then hush, then the storms breaks.

She raised herself very cautiously. Her bed was high, built on this platform reachable only by ladder. It was ingenious, really, invisible and airless. But there was no bedspring to creak. The rooms were still. It could not have been the wind that knocked over the geranium. But she wasn't about to go down and see.

She stayed propped on one elbow, listening to her own heartbeat, her eyes widening as though they would drain all the darkness and discover what waited on the floor.

Suddenly she thought of the men who had moved her from Jane Street. They'd just been an ordinary pair of muscle men, young guys, silent lifting types. But she remembered she'd had to ask the winos to leave the front stoop so her furniture could pass. And when it was all over, when all her cartons, her stereo, her sewing machine, her velvet chair and Swedish rocker had been carried up and placed, after the movers were safely paid, one of the movers turned to her. He had lank yellow hair, she remembered, and wide pale eyes.

"Lady," he said. "Lemme ask you one question. Okay?"

"Okay."

"How come you moved here? You a social worker or sumpin?"

How come I moved here? How come I moved here? The words fit the rhythm of her own heartbeat as she waited in the dark. And then she heard the loft bed ladder creak. I'll jump, she thought. Anybody comes up here, they won't expect me and I'll jump and then it's out the door and down the steps—easy—please God, there'll be no winos on the stoop. . . . Maybe the butcher's dog . . . maybe a policeman. Fat chance. . . . Never saw a policeman yet, not when you need them. . . . "Lady, why'd you move here? Why'd you move here, Lady?" How many words can sizzle through your head while you feel the ladder rock unmistakably and then—there it is!

166

Thud.

The street lamps, the no-shadow crime-detecting street lamps, set a day glow in the front of the apartment. But the loft bed was quilted in shadow. Nothing. NO! And in some trick of the light, suddenly, two wild eyes, two flat discs of light glaring in the darkness.

Then two more! NO!

Fedora's friend!

"Blast you, Fedora! You! Get out of here! Get out of here! Git!"

She jumped up on the bed and the two cats fled, springing off the side. Pam had to come down the ladder, stumbling in the darkness, finding a broom, unwilling to switch on the light and be revealed to the whole neighborhood of window watchers, dying lest she step on those monsters in the dark.

"YOU GET OUT OF HERE!" Charging with the broom till both cats leaped out of the window and down the fire escape like a pair of thieves. Yet she couldn't close the window all the way. It was too hot. I'll have to get a grate. I'll have to get screens. . . . Then how will Fedora get out? And he was just learning to be a tomcat. Poor Fedora, I scared his friend away.

She was so tired, and so mad, and the whole mess struck her as so funny. She could imagine telling the story over and over . . . and tomorrow . . . oh, almost today, I have to get up and be at work. . . .

The May sun walks stilt-legged around the garden. Spinach is beginning and beans and hosts of roses are waiting to flip open when I turn the calendar page. Gaudy roses, I know, will cover the June bushes as lavishly as paper bouquets. Meanwhile the peonies offer their heads, warm and fragrant as small children.

I walk around my garden as it begins the hoop of the blooming year. The evidence will be piling up. I believe, with Emerson, that prayer should be praise and not plea. But to whom else can I turn? I can't order my daughter home. She's not a child. She does not want to come home . . . invasion of cats or no.

She wants her own home.

Well, she has one.

Not by my lights.

But by hers.

Not hers either.

Then what can I do?

What else?

I walk around the rose garden. This year I'm going to gather the rose hips, the swollen seed pods, great with child. I had some idea about rose hip tea. (Pam drinks that, gives it to me when I feel a cold coming.) Rose petal jelly, sachet of rose leaf. . . . There are so many ways the rose comes inside, so many ladylike things she does.

I put my hand on a rose bud and wished for my daughter.

# THE FRONTIER OF SCARCITY

AS THE SCHOOL year draws to a close, I try to prepare my students by bringing the semester's work together. We've started with Thoreau, but that was so long ago, they may have forgotten. I must make him relevant, so they will remember.

"What is the new frontier in America today?" I ask.

Total blank.

"What is a frontier? How would you describe it?"

"Unexplored."

"Mysterious."

"Dangerous."

"Yes. And why do people go to frontiers?"

"For adventure."

"Yes. Anything else? Why did so many Americans seek new frontiers?"

"Because they had to. Because things were intolerable where they were."

"Exactly. And there is a new frontier in America today —the frontier of scarcity. Our ease-mad society has marched to the no-man's land of shortages in fuel, in wheat, in wool, in meat, in land, in water, in clean air. . . . Where do we go from here? Can we settle this new wilderness and coax it to bloom? Can we make a virtue of necessity, find pleasure in hard work, re-invoke the Protestant Ethic?

"Or have we fallen so deep into the slough of consumerism that the final 'disposable' will be our own lives, lives we just won't take the trouble to save?"

I don't usually lecture. I run my classes more on a discussion plane. Students are uneasy. They are not quite sure whether I am blaming them for all the shortages or whether I am saying something they should note down because it will be "on the final."

"What would Emerson and Thoreau say about the energy crisis?" I ask.

"Ah," the sigh is almost audible. It *will* be on the final. Then it's worth answering. And they seem to like the question anyway. Hands wave.

"That we deserved it."

"They warned us not to mess up the world with machines."

"Thoreau said, 'Use your hands. Chop wood. Grow beans.' He'd think it's great to see us scrap our cars and start walking."

"Emerson too. He'd say, 'I told you to be self-reliant. I told you you'd get in trouble if you followed the crowd.' "

"And how do *you* feel about the energy crisis?" I asked.

"We're gathering wood after every storm. My father says we all may sleep by the fireplace this year. I wouldn't mind that."

"I like the house better cold. When it's hot I get sleepy."

"Old ladies have been calling me and asking me to come over and chop wood. I get paid for that."

"Sundays people are getting together at home because there's no gas. That's nice."

"We don't buy bread anymore. Not at 60¢ to 99¢ a loaf. We bake it."

Boys and girls exchange recipes and compare patches they've embroidered on their dungarees. The class begins to swing into one of those exuberant special hours that makes me glad to be a teacher. One student says, "Gas rationing won't bother me. I've got this long hose ready to siphon out the school buses."

We discuss whether this was what Emerson meant by Self-Reliance.

Well, what about this wood chopping, bread making, patchwork embroidery? How come we're so quick with the solutions before the pinch is even on? How come this electronic generation—cradled in cars and companioned by television—is so eager for old-fashioned alternatives? Nostalgia is not natural for young people.

When I was a child, no one wanted to take my grandmother's marble-topped washstands, her florid Oriental rugs, her fruity chandeliers and her dark heavy furniture. My big sister decorated her apartment in Danish "moderne," wall-to-wall carpeting. Beauty had to be "functional." We prepared for a streamlined future with diesel trains and automation.

Today, young people are harking back to their great-grandparents. The drive to old crafts, to housekeeping and handyman skills, the lust for camping in the open air, may have begun as a fad among the youth. But it seems to be contagious. We old folks are in it too. Lusting for a time we never knew, we are growing vegetables in the backyard and on the terrace, herbs on kitchen window sills. We are collecting patches and making quilts for the cold nights to come.

It's as though we are beginning to realize that automation is not the answer, that we've chosen the wrong, the "unnatural" fork in the road. We seem to be looking for the forgotten face of America: collecting old bric-a-brac, copying old patterns, humming old songs, listening, perhaps subliminally to the old philosophers' talk about simplicity.

But we are a practical, non-sentimental people. Hobbies are a dilettante's pastime, not a serious pursuit. Perhaps we still have a Puritan distrust for activities motivated only by pleasure. We want the stern goad of necessity to license our enthusiasms.

Here is where the new frontier of scarcity works. It has provided the impetus for improvisation and the sanction for nostalgia. With our modern conveniences curtailed, we must return to the old lifestyles. We are like small children —aghast, yet slightly pleased to see our house burn down, eager for new adventure. But, unlike small children, we know we were poor housekeepers. We stoked our fires too high, did not clean the chimneys. The current impasse may be the only way to save ourselves from choking in our own waste.

Circumstance has judged us guilty; atonement brings relief. Now our lust for pioneer activities is spiked by the same necessities our forefathers knew. We are alone in a new world, forced to self reliance, menaced by our environment. We can depend upon no outside help. We must cultivate new sources of power: "people power"—our hands, our feet, our eyes; natural power—the sun, the wind. This is the only type of energy that is non-polluting, non-monopolizable, and will never be in short supply. No longer are we playing a game. Our bicentennial may be more than a token commemoration. This time we have to practice nostalgia for real. Can we make it?

There are signs.

Ben's invention, the Franklin stove, is working overtime. Everyone who can is hunting firewood, sea-wrack, storm-wreck. Two handled saws offer great avenues of communication. Vermont state foresters have ticketed trees for cutting; they sell wood for a dollar a cord if you go in and chop it yourself. There is talk of generating electricity from dead wood lying on the forest floor. I just clipped an ad for a solar energy hot water heater.

Newspapers have been running a new kind of story: not just "who killed whom," but "who coped how." I've read about windmill generators constructed over waterfalls, the delivery man who bought a horse and wagon, truck manufacturers forging woodburning stoves out of scrap metal, vacationers safe and convivial on trains instead of scowling bumper to bumper along the highways. A conservation-minded housewife converted to fluorescent bulbs and, because they diffuse a cool light, she is able to cultivate beautiful indoor gardens along with her reduced light bill. The indoor plant business is booming (blooming?) because our lust for nature complements the energy crisis. Plants thrive with lowered thermostats; leaves retain moisture and moist air feels warmer. Billeted among our daily ration of newsprint disasters come these tales of American know-how.

I remember Christmas ads keyed to our exuberance over nostalgia. "Give her a sweater to outwit the fuel crisis." "This winter you're going to walk more. You'll want something warm and lightweight." "Housewarmers—long, toasty robes," superimposed over a sketch of a pot-bellied stove. "The gasless carriage for Sunday drivers—a bicycle." "VW for gas pains."

They say electric consumption is noticeably down compared to the same period last year. Traffic fatalities have been reduced by the new lowered speed limits. Motorists admit driving is easier without competitive speeding. They may even look at the scenery.

We have learned that our planet is too small to provide unlimited quantities of meat. So new cookbooks have come out with alternatives: vegetarian, weight-watchers, casserole, wok, herb magic, etc. We are learning the thrifty food habits of poorer countries and our stores are full of new pots with an old-fashioned glow: tin, iron, copper. In the cold nights ahead our kitchens may glow; our diets may be more varied than the old meat and potatoes.

The "Victory" vegetable gardens of World War II are being replanted in private backyards and communal plots. Seed houses say they cannot keep up with the sudden rush of new customers. Tentatively, city fingers decode weed from seedling. I just read about a city couple who planted a terrace garden and some finches came and built their nest and hatched their birds in the window box. "A miracle!" the people said. "A real miracle—birds in our concrete jungle!" It's as though some buried memory seems to say —yes, this is the way. This is what you were looking for. Progress is not the miracle; life is.

Home will be colder and darker this year. The larder may be low and life won't be easy. But it is quite possible that we may become so tranquilized by activity that our hypertension will subside. Perhaps we will sleep without pills. The smog-freed air may clear our heads and spare our curtains. Sludge may disappear from the sea and fish will spawn again. We will tap new clean sources of power, and we will learn when it is better not to use power at all.

It has been predicted that we would die of gluttony as the Romans did. We won't have the chance. But we might die of sloth.

Or we might, we just might, pull through. Whitman said, "I hear America singing. . . ." With the machines subdued, the rocking chairs returned, we might be able to hear that song again.

We thought we had tamed our environment for once and all. We were resting easy on that knowledge, growing fat, sick with surfeit. Now suddenly scarcity has imposed a new wilderness. Will we let it call out the old unconquerable frontiersman in us? Can we cross this new desert? Do we have the energy to cope with this crisis, to sharpen our responses and re-forge old aptitudes, knowing that if we can make our way across this frontier we may, we just may, reach a truly "pacific" ocean? We may rejuvenate something in ourselves we feared we had lost forever: the faith, the energy and the zest for challenge that have built our country.

Many signs say we can. And we may even enjoy the fight.

# MANY ARE CALLED

PAMELA CALLED.

"Meir—is here," she said.

"Oh?"

"I picked him up at the airport. I was standing a little bit on the side, you know, so that if I didn't like what he looked like I could leave. . . ."

"Yes?"

"But he saw me. He saw me first and he came right to me. . . ."

"Where is he staying?"

"With friends. Don't worry."

"What does he think of Elizabeth Street?"

"What should he think of Elizabeth Street? He thinks it's great."

"Of course. Did you have to sweep any winos from your doorstep or don't they work on Sundays?"

"MO-THER, please; they couldn't be more harmless."

"Or less attractive."

"Goodness, I'll never tell you *anything* . . ."

"Okay. Okay. What about Meir?"

"Ahhhh. We talked for hours and hours . . . about everything. . . . and he paints . . . and he brought me his paintings."

The phone grew warm and smooth against my ear. The dishwasher clattered and then stilled.

Bud was reading on the couch as usual. He knew who was on the phone. "Well," he said. "What's up?"

"Nothing to worry about," I said. "He paints. He came with his paintings. A nice stable young man."

I stretched out on my couch. Jenny the cat stared down from her place on the lamplit pillow. There was nothing we had to say. We had one of those long married dialogues: not a word spoken, everything understood.

We both remembered our first date. Bud had arrived at my house with a briefcase full of poetry and he read each poem to me. My parents were—to say the least—not impressed.

At home now, in our "grown-up" living room, we listened to a Beethoven trio for flutes and hunting horns. Suddenly I noticed an irony in the perfection of Beethoven's musical invention. He had a way of ringing changes on a single musical motif that is far beyond the listener's expectations.

This was not the first time we'd noticed a sort of wry cosmic humor in the architecture of our lives, as though someone were amusing Himself by scrambling our intentions. God works in mysterious ways. The glamorous plans of our intellects were upset by the imperious responsibilities of love. After all, thirty-three years ago we had set out to be a pair of footloose Bohemians and what happened? We promptly became parents—not only simple parents with one accidental portable child who will grow up swiftly and disappear. We had *four:* cosmic joke number two.

Far from being footloose, we've settled here in the suburbs and become so rooted to our house that we may never leave.

And Bud wrote a poem to our son Tom when Tom first began to speak. Bud wrote (we were living in a court apartment then and all you seemed to hear from the other windows was "$600," "$7.50," $78.99," "10% reduction"), so Bud wrote, "What of the first colored handkerchiefs up the magic sleeve of your speech? 'The night person . . . the greasy rain.' (recalling Tom's natural child's metaphors) Tell me, boy, will you learn to say the names of numbers loud and plain?" And what did Tom become? A computer expert, a master of super numbers. He tells them cross-country.

Then have we lost because a greater will than ours seems to be in charge? Hardly. Man proposes and God disposes.

Now here comes the cycle full swing again. You can almost see it turn, hear the gears mesh. We are skeptical about our daughter's future with a struggling artist. We are playing the parents' role, my parents' role.

"Really," said Bud, "don't you think all this is a bit premature?"

Jenny the cat blinked in the lamplight. Her eyes were green and cozy. Like Pam's.

# SUMMER DANCE

MY SATURDAY morning class of "retreads" finished the term with a picnic on the flat sunny rocks of our campus. Apple blossoms snowed and the lawn was tufted with dandelions. As a final assignment all my students had written poems. They were self-conscious but well-rhythmed poems—about washing machines and husbands and rose fever, about getting up in the morning and coming to class, about enjoying the class, and one woman wrote, as well as I can remember:

> *"Does God have a dog?"*
> *My daughter asked.*
> *"If He does, it would*
> *Have to be a very special dog,*
> *One that he could pet,*
> *That would not bite.*
> *Perhaps that's why*
> *He took our dog last night."*

The class hushed. We are an easily moved group on Saturday mornings. The people in the class really seem to want to communicate with each other. The lady who wrote that poem was a bright and ardent feminist, but she has warmth that shines through.

The sun was warm on our back . . . on our wedding rings.

One woman said she had been in a car accident. Two months later she met the man who had towed her car away from the tree and the man had said, "Lady? You still alive? Someone must have been holding you in His hand for you to have come out that car alive." She continued, spinning a dandelion thoughtfully, "So I am grateful for every moment. . . . Life is a precious gift . . . even though my husband is gone and I loved him dearly . . . even though I have my moods. . . ."

She is tense and her voice is low as though it came from a cave. . . . She must've been quite beautiful once. I think the accident has twisted her cheekbone.

We've been a Saturday circle for a lovely semester. I felt we'd made a ring on the face of the water. The class inscribed a Hallmark card that said, "We'll miss you," and as I walked to my car, one of my students tiptoed out to the parking lot. He gave me a lovely coleus with tiny blood-penny leaves. He had cloudwhite hair and sky-blue eyes and cheeks pink with shyness. The coleus is in my garden now—very happy.

The term was over. Pens droned like bees over final exams. The air-conditioning couldn't cope with the pent up anxieties of four thousand students. And then—wwwst!— all over . . . time to put sweaters in mothballs, set out the indoor plants. The cool June moon floated guilelessly over the puffed out sugar maple.

And summer rolled in like a boulder, delighting tomatoes and prostrating roses.

We ate on the vine-greened side porch where the wind blows straight through from the boatyard and the big fishing boat comes in the evening and they call on the loudspeaker, "Plenty of mackerel . . . plenty of blackfish . . . plenty of blues." Depends what's running. Bud and I go round to the pier, climb on the wet deck where the man guts his catch for us and throws the offal overboard to the gulls because our cat won't touch the stuff. Bluefish come big as babies. Carrying them home in their newspaper blankets, I feel like Alice in Wonderland with the pig baby in her arms.

Bud makes soup of what's left over after we fillet. The fish goes in the broiler. We cook together, standing over the double sink together, chefs and hosts to our beloved private clientele. We've come over the hurdle of hassle and reproach. A new tender freedom has grown from the recognition of sharing necessities. We, who once guarded our prerogatives like tigers, do a courtly old world dance of courtesies—and enjoy it! Children come to dinner. We all love to eat and our house is good for summer visiting with the shade and the water and everyone returning (I sometimes think) just to check out old memories. They've done so much growing on these rocks, become so brown and agile and capable, had such fun. . . . The house becomes a museum, a rundown ancestral mansion with no consanguinary ghosts.

The trees wear heavy summer pelts. The ground is burned hot. Beetles sleep on the rose petals. There are very few fireflies, very few butterflies, possibly more birds.

I wish someone would grease the cardinal's rasp. Swallows fly forktailed like scissors. Every year they build their nest in the peak of the boathouse where we get together for "formal" opening—raise the flag. Each woman makes a dish, casserole, salad or dessert, and we gorge ourselves and I resolve to compile a neighborhood cookbook because everything is so delicious. But I never get around to it.

Bud and I swim out to our rock and Father Swan brings his children down the channel past us. He breaks the line of march and swims towards us. Bud breaks a branch. "Be still," I tell him. "Movement frightens creatures."

The swan swims closer, puffing out his wings, narrowing his eyes. "Get off my rocks," he seems to hiss.

I lie very still and stare back. Bud bristles his stick. "Don't, Bud."

"I'm not doing anything."

It is a late high tide, the five o'clock sun shines directly into our eyes, scorching the rock. There is a small rustling in the leaves behind us. It may be a water rat; I hope it isn't.

The swan comes closer and the water laps indifferently round the rocks. Our neighbors hoist sail and set out for a pre-dinner spin. They'll just drift in this late afternoon calm. The heat has brought seaweed to the surface and it floats like mermaid's hair. Sometimes it nets a beer can and loses its romantic appeal.

Then—as enigmatically as he approached, the swan swivels away. He swims after his children, flirting his tail violently, as though he were scolding us. But from the front, I'm sure he looks as serenely triumphant as ever.

"Pin," Bud said. It is summer. We play Spook. "Pain," I said. "Paint," Bud said. When this happens the game usually goes: plaint, plating, plaiting, and then it's over. "Patina," I said, thinking I was very smart. "Captain," said Bud promptly. A great triumph. Who would have thought? To reverse letters around that way in your head is quite difficult. I can think of no way to make a further change. "OK, I'm an 'S'." "No, you're an 'SP'." That means he was able to think of a yet larger word so I am further penalized. "What word is there?" I said. "Paintcan." "That's two words." "It's one." "Nonsense." "Look it up."

We dicker idly, delightedly, playing this idle ping pong with words, our first communion and perpetual feast.

We talk about our children and their marriages and their mates, about our neighbors, about what to have for dinner, about how Jenny would never let us have another cat and Trinka won't let us have any other dogs . . . and will Pamela marry? We think of her walking past the winos on the hot summer dawns when she comes home from work.

She was on the night shift, and, characteristically, had invested that with a kind of spooky reality. The night shift nurse "floats." That means she may be sent to different floors, especially in summer when so many nurses are on vacation. So Pam was sent into the free part of the hospital where the poor patients go, bloody victims of Saturday night brawls. I could see her handing out a sleeping pill, swabbing a wound, floating rubber-soled down the night-lit corridor, wearing the perfume some patient had given her, brooding over a chart, watching dawn flood out of the East River where the fat ladies wilted at their window sills and geraniums flourished. What will the years bring to our free girl?

We want to grasp the wheel of the world and turn it the way those Gloucester sea captains steer their ships through storms. But we are not the master mariners. And perhaps it's just as well. Because I've noted time and again, that in moments of greatest despair, when we were ready to abandon ship, when we'd scanned the horizon and seen no shore and no dove returned—it has always come, just at those moments—a phone call, a letter, a new person, an announcement, a new horizon. . . . Some people might call it luck. I don't. It's happened too often. It seems to me that at the moment when we surrender control of our affairs, God takes over—but first, He insists that we shall have done all we can. . . .

All fans roared in the heat. Trinka lay on the tile bathroom floor. I pulled down the blinds and turned the fan on the dripping ice box; people walking up town shook their heads at one another in disbelief. "Did you ever see such heat? Did you ever see such a spell of heat?" 95° in the city. A robin goes too far out on a limb and tumbles of his own weight. He's lucky he has wings. We move through the palpable heat like fish, swimming. Red tongues of coleus pant like dogs.

Bill and Mick come down to check Tanya with us while they go on a camping trip. Mother-in-law-wise, I am happy to see Mick camping. Bill has always been wild for canoe trips. I remember seeing him go off with another boy on Lake George when he was about fourteen . . . and I still remember how pleased we were to see their canoe come gliding down the lake to home.

Remember . . . remember . . . talking we sift through our fingers the drip castles of memory that the sea always destroys and the tide always returns, while love, indestructible as light, waits behind the clouds. Tanya, at eight months, crawls and sits and pulls herself upright and smiles, all of which we regard as miraculous. And is it not? We give her a bath in the kitchen sink and she plays delightedly with the faucet fountain. She creeps after Trinka like a tiny princess with a monster pet. She reaches out her hand eagerly to accept a flower. And when Bill and Mick come home we all walk down to the beach together and Tanya rides in a pack on Bill's back and she sings with pleasure. Part of the thrill of having a grandchild is watching the role-reversal in your own child. My sober son-the-doctor becomes this tender slave, my son-the-father. He is as happy to be Tanya's pack-mule as she is to ride him. Micki plays great pretend—now you see it, now you don't. Her little daughter holds her tummy and roars with laughter.

Oh, come for a hug and kiss . . . first one finished, come for a hug and a kiss . . . last one finished, come for a hug and a kiss . . . ding dong the ice cream man . . . you're invited to a party . . . there'll be balloons. . . .

Pamela arrived one Saturday for an August weekend. Meir was due for Sunday dinner. So were Janet and Tom Burbank. It would be high tide in the afternoon, a good time to entertain. The garden was obediently blooming. Slipcovers had had their midsummer laundering. Pam had been looking at my living room windows critically for some time now. She'd suggested I get rid of the green drapes and buy something open weave and lighter in feeling. I did.

And now, on this Saturday evening she was walking around the room. She approved of the new curtains, yes. She cut fresh flowers, emptied ash trays, plumped cushions, straightened a chair—all this activity from a girl who is famous for her languor (to put it very politely) at home. I watched her gestures. They looked oddly familiar, but I didn't make the connection. There was not too much sense in plumping cushions and emptying ashtrays in a room where people will be sitting and talking for several hours more, no matter what great event is due the following day.

Suddenly, it hit me. She was like the dog who circles thrice before he lies down in memory of tall grass he once had to flatten when he was a wild dog. And she was like the bird who gathers a bit of straw, a wisp of hair (you never know when you may need them) and tidily tucks all flotsam in a circle of other debris until the construct we call "nest" is complete. That's what Pam was doing—a little nesting dance—without conscious thought—like a bird. Apparently her interest in this boy had awakened something. She wanted to show him her home, and she wanted to make it attractive.

Sunday it rained—those wild sheets of summer rain when lightning cracks the sky so you can see the silver road to heaven, and hear, what to primitive man was the thundering voice of God. The seared illuminated trees flinched.

Meir had walked from the station. His black hair was plastered to his head. His eyes were bright black (like Bud's). And his teeth were white and even. He was about 5'8", Bud's height, and 126 pounds, Bud's courting weight. And he said, "Hello, Hello," of course, smiling sweetly, and then later—"Isn't it wonderful when it storms like this? Then you know Someone up there is in charge . . . someone *very* important."

"Yes, oh yes," I said.

If Pamela said a word all evening, I don't recall it. Only once, when it was a question of seating arrangements at the table, she said—as though anyone had challenged her— "I'm going to sit next to Meir." Once again she moved more swiftly than I was used to seeing her move. Some light had turned on inside her and erased the shadows from her eyes, given a pearly luster to her skin. There was a bright aureole of happiness about her that was unmistakable. It was heightened, perhaps, by the dark, almost Indian, contours of Meir's face, and echoed in the surprising whiteness of his wide smile.

Janet's Tom (a cozy member of the family by now) met with me in quick confab behind the ice box door. We agreed Meir was a definite possibility. . . .

# CHURCH WINDOWS

GOOD SOIL, forests, and the easily navigable waters of Long Island Sound and the Hudson River (both leading to New York Harbor) have made Westchester highly desirable living country. Financiers who could afford the leisurely trip to town lived here in the nineteenth century. The rolling country and many rivers must have made admirable farmland because the soil is still rich.

Once we lived in Levittown where the tract houses were built over an old potato farm, and Levitt had to come in with a mound of topsoil for each house before any lawns could grow. But not so here. We moved in in November when the ground was frozen, and I still remember the spring pleasure of digging in that dark loam, admiring the busy worms and the mesh of tiny roots. Brooks and waterlilies and ducks seem to erupt every time a building stops, as though the natural beauty were irrepressible. The county takes good care of the roads and environs and the straight western shore is always manicured by the shining sweep of river.

Because the land and the location are so good, millionaires have come and left their mark.

Janet lives in Ossining, twenty-five miles up the river

from New York. Driving to her house one evening along
Route #9, just past the Tappan Zee Bridge in Tarrytown,
I noticed a sign that said "Philipsburg Manor."

"That's a place," I said. "That's one of those historical
places."

"Mmmm," said Bud, concentrating on the road.

"There's another great place too—right up the road."

"What road?"

"One of these roads. There's a church with stained glass
windows by Chagall."

"Mmmm," said Bud agreeably, sensing a way out. "Find
the road and we'll go some day." We were off to Janet's for
dinner, and he was hungry.

"If we were in Europe, we'd go," I said.

"Mmmmmm," he said.

Janet's husband knew all about Philipsburg Manor. He'd
been taken there millions of times with his elementary
school classes. He recommended the church, but he wasn't
wild to sightsee either. So Janet and I agreed to meet. When
we get together it's always her house or ours or lunch in a
shopping center. We planned an official trip.

Janet has this thing about her. No matter what you plan,
a light turns on. She makes instant mornings. We made the
date and kept it. After all, why shouldn't we be tourists in
our own country? There are only four sets of Chagall windows in the world—in Switzerland, in Israel, in France and
right off Route #9 in North Tarrytown where #448 climbs
through the wooded Rockefeller estates to a quiet suburban
street, a grassy sward and a spray of elm. The sense of
serene space made us think "church" before we saw the
sign. There is no spire, no cross, only a comfortable dark

stone building with a pointed roof and a bell tower growing among the trees.

The famous windows are protected with an extra pane of glass so that without artificial lighting they are invisible from outside. It was a gray Saturday when we paid our visit, afraid the colors would die in the gloom. But inside was all the more magical. Chagall's stained glass pours as fluid as paint. Without rigid lead outlining, figures and backgrounds share tints. Jeremiah laments on blue earth under a green cloud as the sun drops one ray over his stooped despairing body so that his arms seem to cradle light. That sense of cradled light, I think, is one of those double impressions one gets as one grows older and plays more roles.

I remembered, of course, from holding my own infants, that sense of light newly made flesh. And my last child still walked with me. She is not as tall as I am. We were holding hands as we tiptoed down the aisle. As viewer-art critic, I may not be educated enough to weigh angles or label styles, but as viewer-woman—ah! Chagall is a father, I know, and religion is a celebration of birth and of the sorrow and fear in that blue Jeremiah. I could "feel" the painted windows.

We saw a yellow and brown Elijah ascend to the familiar Chagall stable of slow-eyed one-eyed horses. Gravity was defied. A blue peasant Ezekiel prayed to a cherub tipped out of a cloud. Daniel, ecstatic, flew toward heaven while a bearded young man watched and smiled. A smile drawn on stained glass? How? I don't know. How does Chagall get so much movement into still glass?

Janet and I sat in a dark pew. The church was empty but the vault was filled with music. A young man was practicing the organ. His wife and child sat close beside him. As though it had been purposely planned, the window behind the little family depicted Joel, in green glass mantle, kneeling over his books; wife and child watched, hushed, diminutive. When the music stopped, the child in the church said, "That was beautiful, Daddy." It could have been the painted child in the window speaking.

We looked at a window and saw Christ radiant before a sorrowing blue world. Behind the crucified figure, a shadow of gold spread that illuminated all the panels on the southern side, the Sunday morning side. On a bright day, Pastor Smith said, the very walls turn gold. For us, on that dark afternoon, it was amazing how the colors blazed, as though Chagall or the windows themselves held a fount of radiance that could not be quenched.

But this is not an art show; it is a church. The brilliant Chagall panels must enhance, not distract, from the central purpose. So, above the chancel, where an attentive congregation should be focusing, is a Matisse rose window whose green and yellow simplicities are more conducive to meditation. The green is transparent, revealing a pine tree outside. Where you think you're watching a quiet window, suddenly there is movement, affirming a life in the glass. Perhaps, I thought, this is meant to be the eye of God as witnessed by Matisse, who, as a Frenchman, is concerned not only with mystery and revelation, but with decorative symmetry.

Indeed the window was the last testament of Matisse, completed four days before he died. He worked in bed, mixing his colors, cutting out painted papers, having the design tacked on the wall opposite his bed so that he could make revisions. This window, which he never saw installed, was his final artistic vision: the green that leads to God's trees, petaled with a soft golden light that is sufficient unto itself.

We sat beneath the glass pantomimes. The pine needles flickered. Janet was wearing the patchwork jacket I had made her, a clumsy stained glass for my private chapel. The leather was soft against the dark wood. We listened to the young father play the organ for his wife and child.

But when we turned to go, the turbulence of Chagall blocked the aisle. We faced the giant narthex window where the parishioners had chosen the subject—the Good Samaritan according to St. Luke—as a memorial to John D. Rockefeller, whose sons had commissioned the windows.

Chagall, the Chassid from Vitebsk, had entered the subject with his whole vocabulary gleaming. He worked at his studio in France and then with the glass maker and by 1964 the entire work was taken apart and crated for shipment to New York. I love to think of those bits of fractured angels stowed among all the commercial cargo in the silent hold of some great ship.

The "Samaritan" faces west, toward the river and the sunset. This is the only window where Chagall used red. In late afternoon, the glass must bleed light. This is no place for easy prayer, I thought. Here are no shadows to lull, no familiar symbols to pass idly by.

As we left the church the bell tower sounded the hour. We looked past the elms to the tower, and past the tower to the grey glass sky, as though the bells had chimed from there.

Janet drove back down Route #9 to show me the nursing home where she worked, the beautiful houses along the way, and the one she'd modestly picked out for herself. She did not know that Route #9 is a continuation of New

York's famous Broadway and that both Broadway and Route #9 were first a path trodden by the Algonquin Indians as they hunted from the marshy southern canals that are now bricked under Canal Street in lower Manhattan to the northern highlands and Spuyten Duyvil Creek. I told her. "Really?" she said.

We all blaze our own trails.

Lucky trackers blaze together.

I dropped Janet off at her home.

We stopped a moment to admire the Hudson. We had just visited a monument to our American heritage with its dual thrust to God and Caesar; it's a rich man's church. Now here was our private heritage, so easily reaffirmed.

We watched the gentle yet malevolent lapping of the river against the shore. We could almost see a watermark of war canoes heaped with fish and pelts of beaver, otter and deer; of Dutchmen seeking their fortune, maps with the ink not dry; and then, much later, ice boats and ladies skating in belled skirts in the old winters when the Hudson froze. Beside the accidental city runs the reality of river.

A clock is but a brief tick in eternity. The river carves strange runic rhymes. Read me, it says. See. Listen. Light. Dark. Ripple. Shoal.

Drown the moon.

Raise the sun.

All is past.

All begun.

In the beginning there was water. Before there was dust.

"G'night, love," I said.

"G'night, Mom. Thanks for a lovely day."

"Thank *you.*"

The sun prepared to sleep behind the Palisades, banding

the sky in gold, kindling a wake of old rose fires in the purpling shoals. Windows flame, but the Hudson is a cool path of lilac flowers, gray-washed, silver-etched, where many moons will drown and, drowning, paint a path across still waters as we twin-mooned motorists drive home.

And, watching the gray river preen beneath the blazing sky, I thought of my other daughter—the quiet gray-eyed one and the new light in her eyes. Would her new love last? Would it have the transience or the repetitive constancy of sunset?

Driving south—homeward along the river, I asked the question one more last time: is this the one? The right one? And it seemed to me the long slant wand of the sunset answered, "Yes."

So the long shadows of September reached over my garden and prepared for the autumn burning. Mop-headed marigolds and mums, "Yes, Yes," they say, yellow and burned gold sun colors, flop-headed, "We will bloom forever. Just watch. Have you ever seen yellow so bright? Have you seen how the sun gilds us with its long slant wand?"

The tomatoes were busy, clustered like clumsy grapes, firm, fragrant, the pepper-sweet fragrance that belongs to September. Harvesters can stuff pockets, bring bowls, kneel like acolytes, shadowed.

The book says never let flowers go to seed; that takes the strength out of the plant. So I have been out with my shears every morning before the dew melts and the sun comes up so strong the stem might burn at the wound. But one early morning *last* year I must have missed a flower. Because weeding this summer I found three slender seedlings with pencil-line leaves—three African marigold musketeers. They had made it on their own. They must have fallen from an unplucked head.

I was happy to see them. I'd planted those brown and bushy French marigolds by mistake. Here were my old friends returned, the kind I'd always had since first I had a garden. I watched them grow all summer, bursting finally into soft fire-colored balls. For the gardener with ten thumbs, the marigold always comes through.

The neat rows of spring bulbs and the first careful, weeded summer days are finished. The autumn garden is a tangle. Everything has come through, matted, bloom-heavy, burning. The trees are still full. Cruelly they blot the sun and chill the grass. We move our chairs about the lawn but cannot find the warm rugs of sunlight with which we were wont to wrap ourselves like deck passengers in steamer chairs.

Trinka, as unstealthy as a donkey, walks over the long damp grass, pauses, rocks heavy hip-socketed. In the tangle of vine and shadow, I see a squirrel come to harvest, immobilized, turned to stone, nut in hand. A yellow spider mum, beautiful as an altar arrangement, blooms behind the squirrel whose paws are raised in prayer. The dog advances. The squirrel drops. The dog leaps. There is a crash and the squirrel is halfway up the apple tree.

We sit out on our chairs and talk about Pam's wedding (Yes, it happened. It happened. House full of late roses and early mums). How strange it is that after all her Manhattan glamour she is living in a lovely apartment just two blocks from our house because Meir found a job as a commercial artist just fifteen minutes away in Mt. Vernon, and he said,

"Pamela, why do you want to live in Manhattan? It is so beautiful here, so many trees." And Pamela, our explorer, discovered New Rochelle, began to work in New Rochelle Hospital.

So our harvest is gathered. The long shadows of September cover our yard and prepare for the autumn burning. The linden trees stand imperturbable, sun-devouring. But on the red maple I can see the first stigmata of October. It won't be long.

# SOME THOUGHTS ON AGING

I COULD let it go with "happily ever after" but there is one more problem. I have always felt that my role as a parent was to aid my children in becoming adults, responsible adults. And my definition of a "responsible adult" is a person who can stand up and be counted as a *contributor* to society, both in the larger sense of a professional contribution and privately through a commitment to another person and future generations. In other words, a person who can obey the commandment to multiply—fruitfully.

All well and good. But what happens to the parent whose children are grown? Where do you turn for focus? What do you *do* with your days? So much of my life has been spent following that old Protestant work ethic. I have so keenly enjoyed the pressures of necessity, the ability to meet a variety of demands. What do you do when the demand abates? Rest? I'm far from tired.

I have my job. I love to teach. I love to greet that sea of new faces each semester. Teaching, in a way, is an extension of mothering. But deep in my heart I know that my students are really strangers, that my professionalism is not the "real me," but a role I am pleased to play.

I am a home person. I still live in my home, and we have

a crib and a high chair set up again for visiting grandchildren, and all visits are holidays to me. But even when I baby-sit, this is one remove from mothering. I must learn to be helpful without interfering. I have to give these babies back, just as I must return books to the library. I must give up the driver's seat and sit—not too volubly—in the back.

And I don't quite know how to handle this new role.

One particularly grim November day I was sitting at my desk and there was a huge pile of papers I had to mark and a huge pile I had marked. You know, one of those tasks where you work hours and no visible result appears. Even the sun had a pale grim look, the sky was pavement gray and the trees were wrought iron.

And then I looked out the window again. There is a giant sycamore out there. In summer all I can see is my yellow curtain and the shiny lobed leaves of the tree and a brief lacy sky. Now I could see cars and passersby and the house next door, and the tree was still there, of course—a quite different bare tree, and a tiny poem popped in to my head:

*Dear God, I ask one gift of Thee.*
*Teach me to bear my winters like a tree.*

And I listened to the answer:

"The weak go. They always go. Nature runs no welfare state."

Seeing that tree so proud, how could I ask for pity? Or a handout? But the adaptive remain. With faith there is hope.

"Listen, austere, needle-fingered—old, old, before the webbing of leaf was invented, the conifer experiment still burns green after the frivolity of autumn is gone and only an iron grating of branches fences off the sky. Surely you have noticed the evergreens?"

"Assuredly."

"Even more in winter?"

Even more in winter. Sometimes a low taxus or a spreading arborvitae may completely disappear, mounded in snow like a new grave. When I look at the front of my house after a heavy snowfall, half the shrubbery is gone. Knowing that snow breaks branches, I try, ever so gently, to free my trees. But often they do better on their own. They have been blessed with resiliency. They can manage. My touch is too quick, too rough.

Nothing is more patient than a tree, more supple than a juniper—sturdy and rubbery as seaweed. Now you see it, now you don't. Is it indifference or a quiet intelligence that is confident of seasons, not being butterfly foolish? I think a tree has learned the grace of acceptance and the truth of spring: nothing lasts, but nothing's lost; the only constant is change.

Here am I, come to the weathered end of life. I watch my trees and learn so many ways to greet a freeze. A leaf need not be a quill. That's only one part of the cold magic.

A soft leaf may last the winter if it's wired for change. Holly and ilex run up flags of red berries whose seeds pop open, tempt birds, range far, burst, bloom, die, flower again. No parsimony, no color hoarding, no panic here. Even in an ice storm, when the tall branches—glass-sheathed and brittle—bend like courtiers blocking the doorway they usually flank, I see the berries still shining like rubies in a crystal case. Then, later, slowly, slowly as sunlight, the glittering scabbard shatters and fronds rise again in a movement as unmistakable and as invisible as the movement of hands on a clock.

Always the tree serves a larger order, revolves on some primal wheel beyond haste or despair, knows what should be obvious to a scientific people: there is no end to a circle. The cycle of seasons spins our covenant with eternity, with resurrection and with life.

Deciduous trees retreat in winter, thriftily putting their sap in cold storage. We call a winter tree "barren." But oddly enough, as I look out the window and watch my sycamore, so stark and iron bare without its summer greenery, I notice a new grace. Bare branches admit more sunlight to the ground; mysteries of creeper and terrain are revealed. As I drive to work, I remember that the winter road is lighter, admits more sunlight. Leaves are greedy; like children they have many needs that must be satisfied. Leaves hoard the sunlight and will not let it filter to the road. But the winter tree makes an art of austerity. His needs pared to the bone, he can afford to share the light with the rest of the world. And, in the cold, I am grateful to him.

The winter world is a pen-and-ink drawing—literally, a woodcut—rather than the gaudy canvas of warmer days. The intricate skeleton of the tree itself is no longer lost in a daze of green. Scars appear, broken branches, old nests. Is this like age, I wonder, stripped of youthful illusions and disguises, more intimate with light? Some trees have wooden fingers, knobbed, arthritic, clawing at the frozen sky. And some trees—less battered or less resistant?—are a dance of slender line where sun and wind have called the figures in the square dance of the year.

Perhaps there is some mysterious cousinship between the tree's old bones and my own. "Perhaps," says the tree, "brightness is not all." The old tree outside my window has sustained life: reveals light, blooms moons, bears wind, mothers and fathers and mourns a million leaves.

And now, in winter, the tree bears wind (as we must bear trouble) without the frippery of leaf to worry about. Wind pipes on bare branches, skitters and screams around corners. "Reef sails," the tree says. "Storm rig for winter blasts. Reduce your sail area. No excess baggage for long journeys."

It's not that bad to stand alone.

Roots probe frozen soil, skirt stones, meet with other roots to sew the garden to the lawn. A tree, like all life, feeds on darkness and decay, forages for water, crawls beneath a fence, attempts to hold against the tilting earth. Upright and complicated as a loom, it weaves a shadowed magic with the shuttling sun. So must I also grow from a compost of times past and the blaze of today. Memory is a treasure chest that no one can steal. I can scatter doubloons among my children and my children's children. Indeed, have I not just stripped the dingy paper from the silver dollar blooms, scattered their seeds to the wind and decorated my porch? Gifts. Gifts. Seek, and ye shall find.

Intimate of all seasons, even death, a tree becomes a storehouse for squirrels, pueblo for birds, and banquet for insects. When the rigidities of bark relent and become soft as flesh, softer, friable, the tree returns, already stained to match the earth from whence it came. The message is clear: to give is to live, a gift is a token to immortality.

For many years I have sat by this window and watched my special tree-scape of sky, watched so intensely that I can feel an arterial pull, as though through all our circulatory convolutions we share a common pulse. There is talk of plants listening to people. The best conversations go two ways.

*Am I leaf? Am I tree? How many winters can I survive as me?*
*And how many, in some other guise, serve Thee?*
*I look out the window and I see.*

# EPILOGUE: HAPPILY EVER AFTER

SPIN another year!

Janet and Tom Burbank have moved up to Red Wheel Farm, near Carmel where Tom teaches. They have a lake and a wood and a hammock and a slant view of front meadow where Tom races after his lawn mower. Janet makes apple pies from windfall fruit. Inside their house is all window and real wood panelling, so that after Tom hung their plants from the slant ceiling it looked as though they were living in a tree, a tree with green leaves even on these lengthening autumn days. Janet is wallpapering and slip-covering and studying chemistry; and the other evening, when she drove home from work and turned off the great new highways onto Luddington Road, a narrow old pass between meadows, she stopped her car suddenly. There was a deer standing by the side of the road, watching her —as earnestly as she was watching him. And then she looked further across the field—and saw one of those miracles only silence can coax out of nature.

"You'll never believe it. I saw deer dancing! A whole field of dancing deer! Oh, mother, it's so quiet. I'm so happy . . . and so busy."

Our son Tom is building a new addition over his barn so

that grandparents can come. The child is due any week now. He wants six sons, he says. to help build his generator, dig his pool, shuck his corn, gather his squash and ski down his hill. He wants a family compound where Bill will be the pediatrician and the girls will be the nurses and we grandparents will take care of everybody's babies. Suits us. Bill and Mick are expecting again—end of January.

And Pamela sits on our September lawn and the leaf-sifted light dapples her curly head. She is very different from the girl who used to blow in and out like a wraith, dreamy-eyed and vague as though she were not quite sure who she was or where she was going. Now the curves of her face are sharper, shiny clean, her eyes bright and direct. She is like a photograph that has suddenly come into focus. And she is focused, like the spirit of autumn, on her private harvest, her child at her breast. It is as though she were framed for this, from Liza Jane, her green-eyed red-haired doll, to her high grades in pediatric exams; her gentle voice and the soft arc of her arm have suddenly been certified.

"Look at his toes . . . see his toes . . . see how they flex . . . see his hair. Did you ever see a baby with such long dark hair? In the hospital all the people stopped at his window. I watched them. They said they had never seen such a beautiful baby."

We smile.

"They did, really," Meir says.

Why not? The child's eyes are gray and round like Pam's; his hair jet like his father's. He shoots us a cool appraising glance and then returns to the absorbing pursuit of his dinner.

The air is busy with leaves.

The sun slices a bright rind off the chilling Sound. A colony of herons have come to join our flocks. Sailors are putting their boats to bed.

And in my garden, as though it too were part of the family, plants are reproducing like mad. The tomatoes have hatched little tomatoes, which already have their new little crop of fruits. String beans have sprung up on their own. Last year's broccoli decided to be perennial. A mimosa tree blew over from somewhere. My neighbor gave me some branches of silver dollar and, just as I was wishing I had more, I turned and saw that a silver dollar had come up in our yard: "Here I am. Here I am. Fruitful. Multiplying."

"RRRrring! RRrrrring!"

Dash up the back steps, scattering small harvest.

Tom, our son Tom, announcing the ultimate miracle. How many miracles can you have in one season? The first of his six sons (he'd better clear that number with Darlene) had been born, weighing in at 8 pounds, 3 ounces, twenty-three inches. "Ah Tom, Tom, the number, loud and plain!"

We took the little seven-seater plane to Montpelier, the one that barely clears the lovely changing mountains, and there was another apricot baby with red hair this time, and gray-blue eyes and graceful little hands clasping, unclasping above his head.

There was Tom's familar house—askew for the first time with the paraphernalia for this new person. The great computer sulked, forgotten in the office. "Mother, Mother," Tom called. "Come quickly, you must see this." Of course I must. Have I ever seen a baby bathed before? Not this one, of course. I held him in my arms and showed him his waterfall, his meadow, his rocks, and imagined how it would be when he would walk there with Tom. I knew Tom would be imagining that too.

And in the gray misty Vermont morning, Bud and I walked down the road past weathered barns and the brooding cows and the painted mountains. We wore sandals and walked in warm puddles. We walk Trinka at home, Bud more faithfully than I, for Trinka is really Bud's. But when we are away, wherever we are, we come out of our house like those carved couples on cuckoo clocks, promptly and regularly, and we walk together. Is that my favorite thing? After all the pomp of event and consequence . . . that quiet walk over nowhere-going roads? Perhaps.

In the afternoon Darlene and I went to town and bought little-person things and Tom and Bud babysat and then Tom had a client and he put the baby on Bud's broad King Cole chest and the child promptly fell asleep and in the evening Bill and Micki and Tanya came, and we had what Bill used to call a "baronial dinner."

Next day we gathered tomatoes against the frost and picnicked by the waterfall and Tanya went mad for the wind. She ran across the lawn and held out her arms to catch the wind, lifting her arms to passing birds, experimenting with speech that is fluent Phoenician or pidgin English. She has a passion for Bud, his warm rumbly voice and his white beard. "Because I took care of her that first week," Bud says. "Because I held her so close when her cord came off. She's never forgotten that."

And she has a passion for Daddy, whom she sometimes calls "Mommy," but the words are coming swiftly now, every day more and more words falling like the leaves. You can actually see the language root and take flower. "Ou-

shide, oushide," she says imperiously. And Bill, who loves
to go out, takes her on his back, and he and his big brother
Tom hike up the mountainside like a species of proud camel
and princess.

So each of our children has come home.

Tanya rides the split rail fence. "Hoshee, hoshee," she
cries. Bill mounts behind her, and then walks her very
carefully over Tom's stone wall. Being a pediatrician, Bill
thinks there are an inordinately large number of children
who suffer from accidental disasters, and he is always shadowing this little girl. And then she breaks away and runs
down the road. Run, run, run. He's after her. Later Mick
talks solemnly into an empty telephone saying what a good
girl Tanya has been today, Tanya watching, her eyes big
with delight.

Tom's child rocks in his wind-up swing. Then Darlene
lifts him out and presses him to her soft blue robe and Tom
hides behind a camera and a flashbulb, recording it all so
that one day he'll actually come to believe it.

And then it is time to go. We're going to Portland for a
few days, driving cramped with Osa their dog and Tanya's
car seat in the narrow Datsun, and neither Bud nor I are
narrow. But who cares for the vagaries of space when you
are cutting through the White Mountains in September
when the autumn trees are just beginning to kindle and the
car rocks down the winding road, mountain cradled? Who
cares, when the people with whom you are crowded are the
people you love?

In the car we began to play "I packed my grandmother's
trunk," and Tanya began to cry. "She's sleepy," Bill said.

"Nonsense," I said. "She wants to sing."

Micki burst out laughing. "Have you ever heard Billy sing?"

"I think I'm pretty good," Bill said.

"Sing, sing," she said. "He's not only bad, he's incredible."

"Billy and I will sing a duet," Bud said.

"Oh, oh!" It was my turn. "Do you know when we were first married he used to go, 'Do-TA-dada, da-Ta-dada,' and suddenly it occurred to me—he thinks he's singing something. So I asked him. 'Of course,' he said. 'America the Beautiful. Don't you recognize it? da-Ta-dada, da-TA-dada.'"

Then Bud was off singing—"Oh beautiful, for spa. . . ." Bill joined in and Mick and I, laughing, and Tanya, not crying anymore, but singing along. The white ribbon of the road spooled down the mountainside. The sun ducked behind the looming shoulders of Mt. Washington. We saw two hikers with orange packs. Blue chill air rolled down the mountain flanks and stars took up sentry positions across the narrow ridge of sky.

". . . from sea to shiiiiiining seeeeee!" The men finished; it was our turn. Micki was at the wheel. She began to sing softly at first. I could barely catch it. "He's got all little children in His hand. He's got all little children in His hand."

Oh. I picked it up. "He's got all little children in His hand."

Bud and Bill and Tanya, squashed into the back seat, Osa breathing down their necks, They came on strong and loud and together. "He's got the whole world in His hand."

*A new commandment I give unto you, That you love one another*

*. . . that you should go and bring forth fruit and that your fruit should remain. . . .*

I watched the sharp dear profile of Micki as she steered. She was the first stranger to come into our family, the first to give birth, and now a new life was stirring—not visible yet—but begun. Our little caravan sped from the home of one son to the home of another.

God speaks in metaphors and, yes, sometimes through song and dance, translating his presence and his power into wind, water, roses. Yes. I'm an old hand at reading gardens.

But when the word is made flesh, when the metaphor is birth itself—then and then only, is the message greater than life. For the message of birth is love.

For this we give thanks.

As September tilted the earth toward darkness—and, as inevitably, toward light. We drove east to the sea.